LIGHT 'EM UP: IT'S 4:20!

CRIMINAL PATROL TECHNIQUES

L/CPL. JAMES EAGLESON (RET)

SGT. SAM SMITH

ISBN: 1500215589
ISBN-13: 978-1500215583

Dedication

Let us hear the conclusion of the whole matter:
Fear God, and keep his commandments: for this is
the whole duty of man. For God shall bring every
work into judgment, with every secret thing, whether
it be good, or whether it be evil.

- Ecclesiastes 12:13-14

This book is dedicated to my beautiful wife, Lois. Since the day that you walked into my life I've been the luckiest man in the world. We've shared so much together. We've traveled the globe doing what we believe in and love. Training law enforcement officers is an honor and I wouldn't want to do anything else in this world.

You are my life and my world, and my best friend. Thank you for standing by me through all of the good times and the challenging times that we've gone through together. Thanks for being with me through the many nights I've stayed up late working on all my projects; the many meals that we've missed together as I've traveled the world; the long hours that we've traveled all night on the road to teach another class the following day; and the countless hours of delayed flights (and canceled ones as well). Thanks as well for the many sacrifices we've made along the way to push our profession forward. I want to thank you for taking a chance to give up a great career with DHS and be with me as a family.

To Ashley and Amber for bringing such joy and laughter to my life. You two are truly man's best friend and will forever be the official mascots of 4:20!

To K-9 Chloe for the times we worked together, trained together, and the times that we shared at home. I'm forever grateful that you were my partner.

To Deena, thanks for all of your last minute help and editing!

I dedicate this book to the charter members of The 420 Group, who believed in me and turned my living room and a PowerPoint presentation into an international training company. Thanks for all of the time that you've shared and the knowledge that you've given to our students. The 420 Staff has some of the best instructors in the world and I'm proud to work with you. -JE

This book is written by James W. Eagleson and is taken directly from his experiences during his career as a Law Enforcement Officer and Trainer.

Table of Contents

Preface

I recently went overseas to teach a 4:20 class in Bosnia. I taught officers from three different nations: Bosnia, Serbia, and Croatia. All were once part of the greater country of Yugoslavia. In 1994, after Yugoslavia was dissolved, these ethnic groups - Croats, Serbs, and Bosniaks went to war with each other. Old family blood feuds and even ethnic grievances that went back centuries were reborn. These cops' families actually shot at one another in the bloody civil war that broke out in this former Soviet bloc nation.

I was tasked with teaching 4:20 interdiction methods to these officers from three disparate nations. Knowing the violent and volatile history between these countries, I hesitated to take part in this training.

Nonetheless, I'm so glad that I went and taught these officers my interdiction program. I was very surprised and, of course, taken aback that these officers had the *bond* that I had shared with my early co-workers in law enforcement. They were able to set aside their past differences in order to work together for the betterment of our profession.

Nearly every evening, we played basketball after class. This reminded me of the times that I spent with my law enforcement brothers and sisters when I was at the academy. This was a beautiful thing to see once again. I was able to experience what I haven't felt in a long, long time.

My time in Bosnia has inspired me to keep pushing our profession forward. This is what drives me to try to be the best at what I do. It helps me to stay current and keep learning and passing this information on in my classes.

One of the biggest reasons that I wanted to be a cop was for the *camaraderie*. When I first became an officer, there was a strong bond amongst police officers. This is the same type of *bond* that firefighters still have today.

I can remember my first day on the job as if it were yesterday. I was so excited to go to the police academy so that I could learn everything that I needed to know to be an effective police officer. I learned and absorbed this information like a sponge.

I did so much better at the police academy than any other school that I've ever attended. This was something that I knew that I was born to do. It was in my blood… and I recognized this early on.

I can still remember sitting in the front row at the academy when they handed out this big three ring binder. I thought to myself *"How am I ever going to learn all this material in a short amount of time?"* But I was up to the challenge.

I met officers from all over South Carolina at the police academy. No matter where they were from or where they were going, no matter what color of uniform that they were going to wear, we immediately started *bonding*. It was if we were all part of a very large, extended family.

I can remember that there were four of us connected to a dorm room. We spent hours each day talking. We knew about each other's families and friends. We talked about what we wanted to do with our careers in law enforcement.

Graduating from the academy is another event that I'll never forget. Nor can I forget the day that I drove back to the city of North Charleston and the chief of police pinned a badge on me for the first time. I really did feel that I was *bulletproof* and ten feet tall.

I was immediately welcomed by the veteran officers with whom I'd soon be working. I couldn't wait to see who they'd matched me up with and who was going to train me.

This was exactly why I signed up for this type of work. There used to be "after shift get-togethers" where we'd all go out to eat together. I remember all of the cookouts at a co-worker's house. I can still remember all of the Christmas parties.

It's a shame that these recollections are now mostly distant memories of what we used to have in our profession. These were once great days for all of us.

Unfortunately, there is a current trend in law enforcement where too many cops are too swift to tear each other down just so they can get ahead in life or advance their own agenda. At times, I've seen other officers *step* on their co-workers just because they can. Bullying is not only a problem in our schools, but also occurs in our profession. Careers are damaged and reputations are tarnished from purely selfish motives.

Rarely does anyone host Christmas parties and after shift dinners any longer. Much like the dying embers and coals of a barbecue that's been left unattended, police cookouts and after shift get-togethers have burned out as well. The morale of our profession is suffering because there's little to no camaraderie amongst cops any more.

It's a shame that our profession has gone down this path. Why is it that firefighters still have *camaraderie* and we don't? Can it be because they still eat together and hang out together after work?

I want to challenge you. If you work in an agency and have a riff with another officer, then be the better person and take the initiative to work things out. Take that co-worker out to breakfast, lunch, or dinner and try to settle your differences. My experiences with those officers in Bosnia inspired me to be the "better man" in those situations and to try to influence others the same way.

This has also inspired me to want to do something for my profession…which I did. On April 20, 2013, I opened up the first ever, law enforcement resort in this country. *It's for cops only!*

I wanted to have a place where officers can go to relax, recharge, and reboot; a place where they can take their families. I wanted to make it affordable because I can still remember when I first began my career in law enforcement. I didn't make much money.

I've also made some recreation land available to go along with the cabin. Our guests can now use this property to go hunting without having to book a guide and pay expensive fees.

I wanted to have a place where cops can concentrate on their families away from work. Yes, we do have the best job in the world...but we also have the highest divorce rate of any profession out there.

This also inspired me to write books so I can join with other officers and "make a difference." I hope that this allows them to add more resources to their arsenal. My wish is that we can one day restore this profession to what it used to be and the way it should be. I strongly believe that we all can help by taking the first step.

CHAPTER 1

IT'S 4:20 SOMEWHERE!

My guess is that you didn't enter law enforcement for the pay or for the great hours. So why do we do what we do?

The *job* does offer excitement and each day we don't know what we'll see. We like being in the middle of everything in the "best show on earth." Law enforcement is truly one of the best jobs in the world!

What exactly does 420 mean? The number 420 refers to "National Pot Smoking Day". It's celebrated each year on April 20th. It's a huge festival all throughout the United States (even in Canada). This is a massive event where strangers and friends meet to smoke marijuana. It's all about getting high!

There are many publications on the market about 420. For example, there are monthly published magazines about cannabis such as *High Times,* one of the original publications about "weed."

You can go on the internet and search "420" and discover thousands of websites dedicated to marijuana and subsequent 420 products. There are bumper stickers that say *"It's 4:19, do you have a minute?"* This means *"Let's go smoke a fatty together."*

There's a radio station in Atlanta, Georgia that at 4:20 p.m. every day, the disc jockeys do a time check. For an entire minute people call in and do their best to imitate the voices of people who are stoned.

"It's 4:20!"

"Dude, it's 4:20!"

"Smok'em if you got it!"

Where did 4:20 originate?

San Rafael, California is the birthplace of "4:20." Every day at San Rafael High School, after the last bell rang, kids would meet by the Louis Pasteur statute to smoke marijuana. Someone must've looked at his watch and noted that they met every day at 4:20 p.m. Therefore 4:20 became notorious as the "time to get high."

Later, the California State Senate tried to legalize marijuana. The pro-legalization state senators called this bill "Bill 420." No wonder there are twenty plus states in the USA that have legalized the use of marijuana.

There are several negative things that are also associated with 420 such as Adolf Hitler's birthday and the shootings at Columbine High School that occurred in Colorado on April 20, 1999. It's been said that the birthday of the leader of The Grateful Dead, Jerry Garcia, is also on April 20, but this isn't true. Rumor also has it that Bob Marley was born on 4/20, but this is incorrect as well.

There have been several movies where the number 420 has made subtle appearances. For instance, the movie *Dodge Ball* has a scene where the characters go into a locker room and two guys are seen wearing sports jerseys. One jersey has the number "4" on it and the second jersey has the number "20." Let me ask you "How many people are on a dodge ball team?" I can answer that. There are not 20 people!

The movie *Hot Tub Time Machine* also has a 420 reference. The main characters enter a hotel within the first five minutes of the movie. When the accompanying bellhop arrives at the door and opens it, one of the guys steps back and says "Look, it's the old party room. It's room 420."

You can find 420 events for most towns in the United States. If you Google™ web search the name of a town and add "420" to it, you'll see all sorts of pot smoking events going on in the city. For example, take www.denver420.com. The Denver

420 people have their own canoe trips, camping trips, outings, and festivals. You'll also see signs for 420 parties.

Recently, while looking through a variety of magazines, I've found advertisements for clocks for sale. The time on the clocks was 4:20! While flying across the country and overseas, I've even seen pictures of these clocks for sale in the *SkyMall* magazines.

When Verizon released its new iPhone in 2013, there was a big display in Best Buy. The time on the display was 4:20. I'm sure I can safely bet that if the Executive Board of Best Buy knew what was being displayed by the front door of their business, they'd be pretty upset with their marketing team.

One day, I was watching a St. Louis Cardinals vs. Cincinnati Reds baseball game. I was shocked by an ITT Technical Institute commercial. It featured a gentleman talking to his family about his engineering career. The commercial showed this man walking along a train track. There was a locomotive in the background painted with the number 420. This number was flashed at least five times during this commercial. Even the college's phone number had 420 as part of its digits.

Is there a Highway 420?

Is there really a highway named 420 or is this just a myth? Actually there are highways that are numbered 420 in four states. For example, if you fly into Philadelphia, Pennsylvania, the first road south of Interstate 95 is Highway 420. The other three states that have freeways numbered 420 are New York, Ohio, and Florida

Four-twenty has even gone international. I've had students send me pictures from other countries that had 420 stores. I've been to all 50 states and more than 48 countries. I've also seen these same stores and people wearing 420 t-shirts in other countries.

Here's what's funny. I get a lot of strange looks whenever I wear my 4:20 Interdiction t-shirt. People know what 420 means. In 2013, I went to Bosnia to teach a 420 interdiction school. The Bosnians laughed at me when I told them about 420. They said "There's nothing here associated with this number 420."

Later, I took this class to the Bosnian border to work with them. The very first truck on the very first day was a truck numbered "420." The driver was from Albania and was suspected to be in the Albanian Mafia.

This experience really opened up their eyes. While we were at the border, our 4:20 instructors located a hidden compartment inside a motor coach bus and found a stash of drugs. Within a month after we left, one of our students (Vladimir) hit a major load of marijuana hidden inside a tractor trailer. This netted over 908 kilos of marijuana and set a new interdiction record for the country of Serbia.

Great job, my Comrades!

They now know what time it is.

It's 4:20!

In the last Summer Olympics, the United States women's soccer team won the gold medal. On the front page of the *USA Today* sports section there was a female athlete wrapped in our American flag. She was wearing a headband displaying the numbers 420.

I did my research and she wasn't born on April 20th. What kind of message are we sending to our youths? This female icon, representing her sport as well as this great country, won an Olympic gold medal and had the audacity to display the marijuana reference 420. This seems unbelievable to me.

But on a larger scale, how many people reading *USA Today* never realized what 420 really means? The bigger question is "How many troopers, county deputies and city police officers also don't know what 420 means?"

What about a commercial truck traveling down the highway with the unit number 420 displayed on the side? How many interdiction officers working the interstates might never recognize this truck as it passes them hauling large quantities of marijuana, hundreds of thousands of dollars of drug money, and other narcotics?

Of course, displaying or sporting the number 420 is not against the law. The practical question for officers to ponder would be "How many trucks are in the company's fleet?" It might be highly suspicious if a driver only owns one truck and the truck number is 420.

What about a motor coach bus coming down the highway with the number 420 prominently displayed on its side? The question that you might ask yourself is *"How many buses are in the fleet?"* The next question should be *"How much do these buses cost?"*

Here's the answer: a brand new motor coach bus is priced anywhere from $500,000 to $750,000.

Let's hypothetically say that you've stopped a bus and it belongs to a bus company from Vermont. Do you really think that they have 420 buses in their fleet?

It would be pretty expensive to maintain a fleet of four hundred and twenty buses. It's not against the law to have that many buses, but knowing how much a single bus costs should raise some questions. A large bus company makes more sense if it's located in New York City or a large population state.

Now I want to talk about personalized license plate tags. What are they really saying? For instance, I had a student in Alaska who sent me a picture right after he had attended my interdiction class. The tag read *"1mohit."* This picture was taken by my student after he stopped this vehicle for a traffic violation and made a drug seizure.

Another one that I saw was a personal tag that read *"luvz420"* (love the 420). Again, how many cops saw this car go by and never knew what it really meant. Here are a few more examples of tags that I've seen in the past. They've read *"ecstasy," "special K,"* and *"ridnhi."*

One of my favorites was a tag that I saw when my wife and I were traveling back from Scranton, Pennsylvania. We observed a truck pulling a boat with Ohio tags. On the back of the boat was the numeral four and the number twenty was spelled out, It read "4 twenty."

I sent out an email to all of my contacts and told them to pass it along to every law enforcement contact that they had. I'm still anticipating the day that I might see this boat again. I'm hoping that it reads "Sheriff's Office" on the back instead of "4 twenty." I'm hopeful that one of our officers will be able to confiscate this boat. I'm still waiting for my Ohio brothers and sisters to come through on this.

Asset Forfeitures

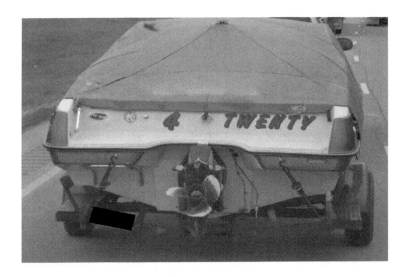

This is about *asset forfeiture*. It's about taking away the ability to transport contraband from these drug trafficking organizations. We want to take away the resources that help them facilitate their criminal enterprise. Seizing their assets will cripple their capacity to transport contraband.

Another friend of mine once sent me a picture of a pickup truck traveling down a Florida highway hauling a dirt bike in the cargo area. It was a racing dirt bike with the number 420 flagrantly displayed.

Racing dirt bikes usually have only two numbers. Again, this was highly suspicious.

Imagine that you've stopped a tractor-trailer that's paid off and you discover contraband hidden inside the vehicle. You just stopped a $140,000 tractor-trailer for a traffic violation and located a load of narcotics. This truck will now be *seized* by your department and sold at an auction. You just took away a drug trafficking organization's ability to transport more contraband. Your department will financially benefit by selling this vehicle and the money will go into your asset forfeiture program.

"Head Shops"

Most towns have businesses which I call "head shops." These shops sell drug paraphernalia such as pipes, bongs, rolling papers, and fake stash hides to conceal contraband. They sell shirts that say "Take the high road," "Highway 420," and several other marijuana references. For example, you may find a t-shirt with a "Cap'n Chronic" caption parodying the cereal brand "Cap'n Crunch." These head shops sell many types of these clothing items, key chains, and bumper stickers, all with drug references.

Myrtle Beach, South Carolina has a 420 store located on Highway 17, just north of the city. I recall teaching at the South Carolina Criminal Justice Academy. I was told that the Myrtle Beach Police Department had one of the highest turnover rates of employment out of all of the police agencies in South Carolina.

Most students at the academy are from the Myrtle Beach area. While talking to some of the Myrtle Beach officers, I asked about the 420 shop. The majority of the officers did not know about the store or its reference to drugs. Again, I wondered how many police officers have driven past the 420 shop and never knew what type of merchandise that it sold. Once when I was off duty, I pulled into the store's parking lot and parked my Crown Vic in the back. I walked inside the store and immediately noticed that my face was on their camera. I looked around the store and in less than a minute I heard the store's phone ring. I heard "Uh huh… yes…uh huh… Okay!" Then I was politely asked to leave… but not before I saw all of the things that they sold.

On February 2, 2014, the Denver Broncos played the Seattle Seahawks in Super Bowl XLVIII. The teams were from two states that legalized the use of marijuana. Shortly afterwards, I was watching *The Tonight Show* and Jay Leno, just before he retired, said in his opening monologue that he heard that the NFL was thinking of replacing the name Super Bowl to the "420 Bowl." He was referring to the states where the Broncos and Seahawks were from.

On April 20, 2013, there was a big "burn off" celebration on National Pot Smoking Day in Denver Colorado. Most people who smoke marijuana will tell you that it's a drug that's all about "peace and love." They'll tell you that those who smoke pot don't get violent after using marijuana. They claim that it's a "mellowing" substance.

Well, as Paul Harvey used to say "Here's the rest of the story". This celebration ended with gunfire!

I watched the chaos on the evening news. These pot smoking, "peace lovers" were running around like cockroaches who had just been sprayed with a giant can of Raid; so much for all of the "peace and love" that was supposedly being celebrated on that day.

I retired as a drug interdiction officer for the South Carolina State Police. As the years went by during my time there, they changed the name from "drug interdiction officers" to "criminal interdiction officers." In an attempt to be politically correct, most law enforcement agencies have changed the name of drug officers to "Criminal Interdiction Officers." Nonetheless, when I worked for the state police, *drug interdiction* was a big part of what we did. Merely changing the name of our unit did not mean that we made any fewer drug cases.

The 420 Group

In 2007, my wife and I founded a training company. We contemplated several potential names for our new upstart business. We wanted a name that included "drug interdiction" but was not limited to only drug interdiction. We came up with "The 420 Group." We are the *Drug Group!*

From its inception to date, we've taught over 370 classes for the Drug Enforcement Administration, Northeast Counterdrug, Regional

Counterdrug, Midwest Counterdrug, HIDTA Groups, multiple state police academies and the U.S. State Department. We've taught more than 500 classes since our commencement. We're now a global company! It's humbling to think that "The 420 Group" started out in our living room.

420 Tattoos

The tattoo market has changed dramatically over the last decade. More than fifty percent of people under the age of 30 now have tattoos. Long gone are the days when a person used to walk into a tattoo shop and pick out a design from a flash art chart on the wall. Today, the majority of tattoos are custom designed and personalized. The tattoo artist will work with his client to design whatever the client wants. Usually it's something that's meaningful to the customer like a child's name, a religious icon, or military insignia. The tattoo signifies something important in that person's life. Therefore, if you see a tattoo of a marijuana leaf or the number "420" inked on someone's body then you can safely conclude that "smoking weed" plays a significant part of that person's life.

I like to ask people about their tattoos and why they've put ink on their bodies. I want to find out what the tattoos represent. I also like seeing tattoos of area codes on bodies because it tells me where a person is from. For example, say that you're dispatched to a suspicious person selling narcotics as he's walking down the street. You arrive and find a bare chested, shirtless suspect. You can plainly see a

420 tattoo on his pectoris and a marijuana leaf on his shoulder. The number 209 is tattooed on his neck.

What do the tattoos tell you?

The suspect has no identification. He only gives you a name and a date of birth. However, you know a little bit more about this person then what he's reluctantly decided to give you. You know that 209 is an area code for Northern California and that 420 is meaningful to him. Subsequently, you can safely assume that you've located the marijuana-dealing suspect that you were dispatched to look for.

This isn't 100 percent, but at least it's a good start. Get a phone book and tear out the page that lists the area codes and keep it inside your squad car. Knowledge of area codes will help you as you're doing this kind of work.

I've seen multiple 420 tattoos over my career. I once taught a class in Phoenix, Arizona and went to lunch with some of my students. When our waiter saw my 420 shirt, he said to me, "Dude! That's a cool shirt! Right on, man!"

I looked at his right arm. He had a tattoo of a clock and the time was set on 4:20. Then he suddenly became nervous after he read "criminal interdiction" under the 4:20 logo on my shirt. He was so shaken up that he dropped his tray of food.

I said to him, "You must've smoked a lot of marijuana in your time to have a clock stopped on 4:20 tattooed on your arm!"

"Yeah… I used to, but I stopped smoking it two weeks ago," he replied.

The waiter was from Columbus Ohio and I don't believe that he stopped two weeks ago.

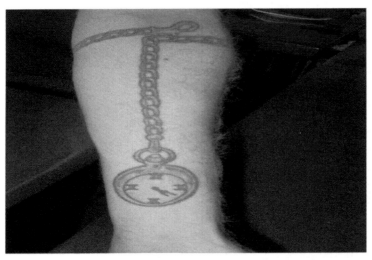

I have many, many more stories and cases referring to 420. If you have any 420 tales, seizures, or experiences please send them in to us. We always like hearing these stories.

Remember, it's always 4:20.

CHAPTER 2

CRIMINAL INTERDICTION

What is criminal interdiction?

Criminal interdiction is about going out there every single day and diligently working your eight hour shift. It's about getting off of your cell phone and being vigilant.

What did we do before cell phones? We were *proactive*. We enforced the law and worked the streets like we should. With today's technology, it seems that every time you turn around, an officer is on the phone or on a computer. Technology is a great tool, but it's often a distraction from our main goals.

Criminal patrol is about working the streets and seeing things that untrained officers are not seeing. It's about learning your area and knowing what's right and what's wrong. Once you have training in criminal interdiction you'll be able to see these things more clearly.

Sometimes the obvious is not so obvious.

It's not just about the big drug seizures. It's about going out there every single day and getting into something new. It might be counterfeit CDs today and it might be a stolen vehicle tomorrow. It's about being a well-rounded officer and -once again- being able to recognize the things that don't seem right. Of course, we like seeing the *big money seizures* since they fund our department's asset forfeiture accounts. These seized monies can be used for training and equipment. This helps your department's annual training budget so you can spend that money on other items.

As we know, all too well, you don't have to put on a military uniform and go overseas to fight the War on Terrorism. It's here in our country right now! Each day, there are terrorists driving up and down our interstates.

They're staying in local hotels in small towns. They're traveling great distances and stopping to eat at fast food establishments just off the interstates. Our country's first line of defense is the interdiction officer; the proactive officers who come to work each day and try to make a difference.

I predict that new officers are going to see more drugs than ever before. With twenty-one states that have now legalized marijuana, drugs are traveling down our highways even more than ever before.

The Drug Enforcement Administration (DEA) has several warehouses on our nation's borders filled to the brim with marijuana. I toured the DEA warehouse in Arizona. There was over 200,000 pounds of marijuana locked away inside. You could smell the cannabis several blocks away. This was just one warehouse out of several. This doesn't even include the Department of Homeland Security's warehouses.

Interdiction is about high-volume stops, stop after stop, all day long. Think back to when you were taught how to use the radar. Think of the steps that you had to follow. You had to visually estimate a vehicle speed. You had to go out on a highway and sit there and watch traffic drive past you.

officers and departments. Interdiction is about sharing information with others. It's not about *glory* or getting your name in the newspaper.

It's also very important to have a good partner and have strong support from your supervisors. You should make it your goal to get your supervisors to attend the same classes that you take. This way it's easier to explain the things that you're seeing and they'll have a better understanding of what's going on with your cases.

I was lucky to have supervisors that took the same classes that I did. They could defend me whenever I received a formal or informal complaint for doing my job. They could read my reports and get all of the information that they needed to answer these complaints.

It's also important for you and your team members to be on the same page whenever you're working criminal patrol. If you're a proactive cop, working an eight hour shift and plan on making lots of interdiction stops, then it's best for everyone to be on the same page.

For example, say that you make a vehicle stop that leads to a drug seizure. A couple of your fellow officers are curious so they stop by to see what you have. To your surprise, and complete disdain, these aloof officers start cussing at the suspect and it's recorded on your video camera. These officers are fully aware that this case will go to trial. Of course, this conduct is improper and does not look good in the eyes of the jury. As if things couldn't get any worse, one of your unprofessional colleagues makes an "off color" comment that could offend anyone…including a jury member. If the other officers are not needed, then it's essential that you tell them to move on and you'll talk to them back at the station.

There are a few other things to consider by having fewer officers on a traffic stop. The last thing that you want to do is have eight officers on a traffic stop (with one violator) and then ask for "consent to search." You need to remember that if this case goes to court, a good defense attorney will make a motion to suppress.

Consent has to be *free* and *voluntary*. Eight officers on a traffic stop can look intimidating. I'd suggest that if you're going to search a vehicle then you need to have only one officer to watch the violators and another to help search the vehicle. The backup officer *never* searches the vehicle. I'll cover more of this in the Chapter on Traffic Stops.

Be sure to make every traffic stop a potential "interdiction stop." It doesn't matter if a person is sixteen-years-old or eighty-years-old. It also doesn't matter where they're from. Treat all contacts the same.

Take your time with every traffic stop. If you preload your traffic tickets before making a traffic stop, then you're possibly missing criminal indicators. If it takes you one minute to write a traffic citation then you only have one minute to be suspicious and develop your probable cause.

Think about how many times that you've heard of an officer stopping a vehicle and making a drug arrest and seizure only to find another officer's traffic ticket inside the vehicle. The date of the citation confirmed that this car and driver were stopped just prior to the arrest and drug seizure.

This happens more often than I'd like to admit. I don't understand the mindset of pushing traffic tickets for revenue. There's more money to fund your department when officers are working drug interdiction.

Here is the duplicity of this type of thinking. We have terrorists in our country. *And we're worried about traffic tickets?* We have to change the way that we conduct business. We have to be more "proactive" than "reactive." Interdiction efforts are making a huge difference in police work.

CHAPTER 3

PRE-PATROL PREPARATIONS

Pre-patrol preparations are very important and should be learned before you ever start working criminal interdiction. This chapter will set the order of things that you'll need to do before you hit the streets.

As law enforcement officers, we should keep everyday goals in mind. Our top priority should be the determination to safely return home, each and every night, to our families. Another goal is that we should never embarrass our profession. We should not violate people's constitutional rights and be mindful that we took an oath to "serve and protect."

When should you start thinking about your next felony arrest? I hope the answer is "Now!" Keep in mind that most crimes will involve a vehicle at some point. Eighty percent of all crimes involve vehicles! The correct response to crimes and cars, as law enforcement officers, is to make a high volume of traffic stops.

You have to prepare today in order to be prepared for tomorrow. If you're going to do this kind of work then you have to be organized and equipped!

I know that you want to be the best at what you do. I know that I do! The day that I think that I'm not the best at what I do is the day that I'll hang up my hat and stop teaching. This is your profession too! It should be your goal to be the best at what you do.

Let me tell you something that you haven't heard in a while. You are the best at what you do! I want to say this again. *You are the best at what you do!* I want to thank you for your service and I truly appreciate you and what you do.

What's in your Resume?

First of all, you need to establish your background and have a "rolling resume." List all of the classes that you've ever attended no matter whether you think that they're important or not.

These are your training hours, so add them up. Your resume is very important so that when you go to court you'll have a list of all of the courses that you've ever attended.

The last thing that you want to do is go into court without your resume and talk about your experience while leaving out all of the schools that you've ever attended. Don't rely on memory and sell yourself short!

Life Experiences

Also list all of your life experiences. Let's say that you were an EMT prior to a career in law enforcement. Your expert testimony will count in court if you've witnessed someone who's overdosed on narcotics. Testifying that you've treated someone who was seriously injured by a drunk driver carries a lot of weight with a jury as well.

Know your Jurisdiction

It's also important that you know what's in your jurisdiction or any area, for that matter, where you'll be working interdiction. This may seem kind of trivial, but these are things that'll help you.

For example, let's say that you're a road officer and you have a partner who's a K-9 officer. Do you know which veterinarian treats your partner's canine? Do you have immediate access to the vet's phone number? Do you know if the dog has allergies? Is the canine currently on any medications? These are important things to know in our profession when working with K-9 officers. The last thing that you want to do is lose your canine.

Here's another example. Let's say that your partner's canine is searching a vehicle and accidentally ingests dope. What's the one thing that you could possibly do to help save this dog's life?

The answer is keeping a fifty cent bottle of hydrogen peroxide inside your car so you can pour it down the dog's mouth. This could save his life! Hydrogen peroxide will pump out a dog's stomach and buy enough time to get the dog to the vet's office.

I'd strongly suggest that if your partner is a K-9 officer then you *should* attend as many canine training days with them as possible. It's very important to be on the same page as your partner and understand the dog and K-9 handler's training.

Establishing Business Relationships

Do you have a business in your jurisdiction that has a garage or a lift? You'll need one if you're working interdiction and run across a vehicle that may have a hidden compartment in its undercarriage.

Think about how many law enforcement t-shirts and coffee mugs that you have sitting around your office. Take these items and go out and network with these local businesses. Give them away and establish friendships and relationships with these business owners. This way you can ask for their help later. For the most part, the general public likes law enforcement and is willing to help us. All you have to do is the legwork. Go out and network! Now, I'd also recommend that you do not take advantage of these businesses and only use them when necessary.

It's also a good thing to network with a tire shop. Drug trafficking organizations are still using tires to conceal their contraband. Keeping a local tire shop on board to assist you with breaking down a tire will be a big help to your interdiction program.

The last thing that you want to do is cut open a tire on the side of the road and be wrong! Your program just purchased a tire for the person that you've stopped. If you get several of these complaints, then it's highly likely that your chief or sheriff will shut down your program or replace you with another officer.

Do you have a warehouse close to you that has a forklift operator? What if you stop a tractor-trailer and your canine alerts on the semi-tractor? Do you have a plan in place to be able to offload the cargo inside the trailer?

What about cold storage? What do you do if it's 90 degrees outside and you have a commodity that must be refrigerated? Do you know of a place that can assist you with cold storage?

Even if the driver is "dirty" and is going to jail, you still owe it to the company to maintain the integrity of the load. The professional thing to do is have a place to store the product until the company can make arrangements to pick up the trailer.

What about livestock? Do you have a place to offload cattle? You need to think about these situations if you're going to work interdiction. These questions that I've brought up have been passed down from interdiction officer to interdiction officer over many years. We have to learn from our mistakes…or learn from other's mistakes so that you don't repeat them.

Here's another query. What if you stop a load of cattle and the temperature is 103 degrees outside? You've discovered that the driver is operating on a suspended driver's license and you've found contraband inside his vehicle. What are you going to do with the livestock? *Remember that the temperature is 103 degrees outside.*

Would you call for the local fire department to come out and cool off the cattle with cold water?

This is a scenario that actually happened in the 1980s down in southern Florida. The deputy called the fire department and asked the firemen to spray down a load of hogs. An entire semi-tractor trailer load of pigs went into shock and died.

This would be an awful day for your interdiction program. The sheriff's department had to buy the entire shipload of pork. I bet that the jail inmates ate really well over the next couple of months; bacon for breakfast, ham sandwiches for lunch, and barbeque pork and ribs for dinner.

Here are a few items that I recommend that you keep on you or inside your cruiser while working this job.

Search Gloves

Get a good pair of search gloves. Never stick your hands into something or somewhere that you cannot see. Also make sure that you have a plastic biohazard box inside your trunk just in case you find used syringes during your search. You can properly store the hazardous needles inside this container. You can pick up a biohazard box at your local hospital.

I can clearly recall the time that I worked in Florence, South Carolina and a trooper found a used syringe while searching a vehicle. He secured the needle on the passenger's seat inside his car. Later the trooper absentmindedly placed some paperwork over the top of the syringe and accidentally stuck himself with the needle. He was exposed to hepatitis.

Floor Jack

Keeping a floor jack in your car is another great tool. You'll soon discover that most hidden compartments can be seen from the bottom of the vehicle. A floor jack will allow you a better view of the undercarriage of the vehicle.

Cameras and Cell Phones

Now I want to talk about cameras. Most departments issue their interdiction officers a 35 mm camera or a digital camera. Make sure that you use this issued camera for work only. Do not take this camera on any family outings or vacations. Keep in mind that digital cameras will sequentially number its pictures. Let's say, for instance, that you've made a traffic stop and discovered contraband inside the vehicle. You take out your department issued camera and snap quite a few pictures of the seizure, indicators, and contraband. At the end of your shift, you go home and officially start your family vacation.

On your vacation, you take this camera with you and use it quite liberally. You take snapshots of your kids, different sites, and even a few cute pictures of your spouse in a couple of risqué poses back at the room. After a weeklong vacation, you come back to work and return to the impound lot to finishing taking pictures. Afterwards, you submit these pictures into evidence. There's now a gap between the date on the pictures of the seizure and the day that you returned to the impound lot.

The prosecution will want to see *all* of the pictures and wonder why some are missing and out of sequence. *This does not look good.* It appears as if you're hiding something. What may prove to be even more embarrassing is if the defense attorney subpoenas the missing pictures. Some of these photos may be awkward for someone outside your family circle or friends to view.

On a similar note, I want to talk about cell phones. Do not use your personal cell phone to take pictures of a roadside seizure! Bear in mind that if you stop a vehicle and take pictures with a personal cell phone, then your cell phone can be subpoenaed and entered into evidence by the court. Your personal phone numbers, pictures, and text messages can now be viewed by the defendant's lawyer and any drug cartel member that you arrested.

Flashlight

Make sure that you always have a great working flashlight. It doesn't matter if you are working day shift or night shift. You still need to have a flashlight with you. You may have to look for fingerprints and dust disturbance on a roadside stop. *Therefore, you're missing seizures if you're not using a flashlight!* It's worth your time and money to go out and buy a good quality flashlight. Better yet, use your department's asset forfeiture account to purchase the equipment that you need and want.

Packing Meals and Snacks

Another good idea is to always pack your lunch every day or keep nutritional bars or granola bars inside your cruiser. You never know if you're going to be stuck somewhere for several hours.

I once worked hurricane duty in Myrtle Beach and directed traffic for eighteen hours. I was supposed to be relieved after a regular shift, but this never happened. *Can you imagine directing traffic for eighteen hours?* Nevertheless, the American Red Cross did show up and brought me a warm bottle of water and a sucker that read "Have a nice day."

I should've been prepared. The sucker was gone in two licks.

Dog Leashes

Go to your local Dollar General Store and buy a couple of dog leashes; a small one and a big one. This is in case you stop someone with a dog inside a vehicle and the owner claims that he doesn't have a leash.

Here's what I know from the years that I worked for the state police. If I ever got a dog out of the vehicle and it ran off and was hit by car then I would've been in big, big trouble.

People are attached to their pets. Losing a beloved family dog on a traffic stop could be a public relations nightmare that would make the evening news and very few people would forgive or forget.

Always be prepared for these situations. Remember that these dog leashes only cost a dollar. This is a very small investment for a big pay day down the road.

Extra Car Keys

Here's something else that you might want to reconsider if you're working with a partner every day. Get an extra set of keys to each other's patrol vehicles. You never know when you or your partner may get into a foot pursuit. An extra set of keys will make the job easier, especially if your vehicle is a great distance away.

A Full Gas Tank

Never let your gas tank fall below a half tank. If you get into a high speed pursuit and chase the suspect vehicle a great distance, it'd be embarrassing to run out of gas. This has **never** happened to me in my career (okay, it happened to me twice and was very embarrassing).

First Aid Kit

Many law enforcement agencies will issue First Aid kits to their officers. If you take something out of your First Aid kit and use it then make sure that you replace it. Oftentimes, cops get in a hurry when they use their First Aid kits, but fail to replenish the items that they've used. There have been several times that I've opened up a First Aid kit and discovered that half of the kit was missing. This is a terrible realization; especially, if you need to provide first aid to a fellow officer who's been injured.

Umbrellas and Raingear

Extra raingear is always a good idea as well as keeping a couple of umbrellas inside your trunk. The umbrellas are not for you. Let's say that you make a traffic stop and get consent to search a vehicle. Out of nowhere, it begins raining, so you decide to put the driver in the backseat of your patrol car. Why is this a bad idea?

Consent can be withdrawn at any time and if the driver is in the backseat of your patrol car then he doesn't have the opportunity to retract his consent. A consenting driver cannot withdraw his consent if he can't talk to you. Therefore if you want to win in court, don't put the driver in the back of your cruiser because it's raining. Provide him with an umbrella or raingear instead.

Know your Environment

Always choose a good working area if you're going to be stopping and searching vehicles. Get to know your surroundings.

When I lived in Florence, South Carolina, one of the areas that I liked to work was approximately a mile from an exit that had no facilities. Consequently, if I stopped a driver for "speeding" and pulled him over right before the exit, I'd structure my questions and carefully listen to his answers. I'd become immediately suspicious if the driver told me that he was taking that exit to get gas. Remember that I mentioned earlier that this exit had no facilities. If this happens to you, then make sure that you look at the gas gauge. If it is half-to-three quarters full then this could be an indicator of criminal activity.

Make sure that your working area has wide shoulders on the roadway. This could prevent you from being hit by oncoming traffic. Make sure that you're not pulling cars over next to a guardrail.

Leave room between you and the car in case you have to make a quick escape.

Try to work an area that has a wooded area in the middle of the median between the two lanes of highway. This could prevent head-on collisions.

Position all four tires of your police vehicle in the grass and turn your steering wheel out towards the roadway. The tires should be pointed out towards traffic. This way, if someone hits your car from behind, it won't be knocked into you while you're interviewing the driver. It will be forced into the highway and should not strike the car that you've stopped.

Try to mix up your hours and work all three shifts. Neither should you get into the habit of working the same geographical regions all of the time. Try to keep the bad guys and smugglers always guessing where you'll be working next.

If you're working nights then try to make your stops in areas that are well lighted with streetlamps. If you're working an interstate near a town or city then work the region that's the gateway to the city because there'll be plenty of lights to help you.

Cops always seem to like complaining that they never have backup or there's never an available canine. They'll even complain that the callout time takes too long.

Here are some ways to help you. Try working closer to where your K-9 officer lives and can respond within ten to fifteen minutes. Now don't go working your interdiction within two blocks of the officer's house. I'm just saying, "Why work at the opposite end of the county when you know it is going take a long time for the officer to respond?"

The same thing goes for your backup officers. Work close to them so that they can get to you within a reasonable amount of time. Here's a thought. Did you know that you're actually in control of most of the things that can make your job easier?

I always preferred working on the edge of town when I ran interdiction on the interstate or a back highway. This way, I was close to the county jail, judges, headquarters, backup officers, and K-9 officers. Neither did I have to wait very long for a towing service.

I liked to make a case and get back on the road as soon as possible. Nothing was worse than working 30 miles away from the jail or even further away from a towing service. I'd have to sit there and wait ...and wait ...and wait.

If you're doing this then you need to change your ways and manage your time better. Time management is very important in nearly everything that we do. I guess that the only thing left to do in a situation like this is to finish all of your paperwork so after you've transported your prisoner to jail you're ready to go get another one.

Tools of the Trade

Now that you're almost ready to hit the streets the next thing that you need to do is get the right tools. You don't need a lot of tools to work interdiction, but there are *certain tools* that you need to keep in your arsenal.

Our profession is unfortunately similar to that of school teachers. We have to pay out of our own pockets for the things that we need in order to do our job more effectively. I don't agree with this! I believe that police departments should supply their officers with the things that they need.

I was lucky enough to work for a department that was very supportive and provided us with the essential things that we needed to do our job. I had a lieutenant who used to be a sergeant major in the army. He took care of his troops and he took care of me. Thank you, Lt. Hooten.

There are several interdiction tool kits on the market. We sell one on our website that comes in a bag with all of the tools that I used to carry on the road. This is the same kind of tool bag that I take to all of my classes. The instructors of "The 420 Group" and I have searched thousands of cars and we haven't had to get any additional tools to complete our tasks.

All you really need are just a few items like an open end tool with a set of bits and an upholstery tool known as a Crow's Foot. These items cost about ten to twelve dollars apiece. However, I want to emphasize that *you* are your "best tool." With a little practice, you'll soon discover that you can take just about anything apart. When I first started in interdiction, I was awful at turning a wrench. I had to practice with it. You'll need to practice with these tools as well.

Go to a junk yard with your tool kit and start learning how to disassemble factory made dashboards and other car parts. Believe it or not, the hardest thing about taking something apart is putting it all back together the way it was before. Therefore, you'll need to come up with some type of system.

Nearly everything in the interior of most modern vehicles is constructed of plastic. This makes it easier to remove panels than ever before. We'll cover more about vehicles in the chapter on concealment.

Here are a few things that I highly suggest doing before you start working criminal interdiction. I've taught in nearly all fifty states and all over Europe, the Balkans, and Asia. What worked for me in South Carolina might not work for you.

Meet with your Prosecutor

You should try to arrange a sit down meeting with your local prosecutor. Discuss what you need to do in order to make better cases. Ask what the prosecutor's office needs from you to get easier convictions. You and the prosecutor must be on the same page when it comes to criminal interdiction. Ask the prosecutor how he or she wants things done. For example, when should you ask for consent? Do you ask for consent during the stop or after you hand back the violator's license and vehicle information and say, "You're free to go."

I've taught classes all over the country and I've asked officers from the same department this very question. I've discovered that there was no consistency. These officers admitted that they've asked for consent in a variety of ways. Everyone needs to be consistent with their traffic stops. Do me a favor and look up *South Carolina vs. Williams.* This is a great reference to review on traffic stops.

Meeting with your prosecutor will prove to be valuable to your interdiction program. It's also in your best interest to politely correct any coworker that you might see doing things wrong. Case law affects everyone no matter where you work.

Here's another suggestion, if you back up another officer from a different department and you see or hear him doing something wrong, then take him aside and correct him. We're all on the same team.

Don't leave the traffic stop and start gossiping about these officers and how uneducated they are. Don't go around talking about how they're screwing up their traffic stops. I've seen and heard this firsthand. These officers might not be aware that they're conducting business the wrong way. Help them! Our goal is to put bad guys away and take drugs off the streets.

Please take notes about what you want to ask your prosecutor while reading this book. I'll give some good examples to help get you started. By the time that you finish this book you'll have an excellent list of questions.

Here's something to ask your prosecutor. What do you do if you stop a pickup truck that's pulling an enclosed trailer? Say that you see some items of interest that you've seen before that have led to drug seizures (*training and experience*). So you call out a K-9 officer to do an air sniff on the pickup and trailer. The police canine gives a positive alert, but only on the trailer. What do you do? Can you search the pickup too? What *can* you do?

Here's something else to consider. Say that you're a city cop and you're working one mile of the interstate that runs through your municipality. You observe a moving violation, but you stop the vehicle outside city limits. You see several indicators that lead you to believe that criminal activity is in the works. You issue the violator a warning ticket and give back his information. You tell the driver that he's free to go, but before he pulls away, you reengage and ask for consent to search.

What just happened here? You probably guessed it. The vehicle is out of the officer's jurisdiction. This happens more often than you think.

Here's another problem that I've seen occurring over the past several years pertaining to traffic stops. It's apparent that officers are not familiar with criminal traffic code. For instance, let's say that you like stopping drivers for "crossing the center line" or "driving left of center." You use these violations to make contact with drivers and passengers to develop probable cause for your interdiction efforts. Then you need to read this section of law again.

I've reviewed this law in a variety of states. Some laws read that in order to stop and cite a person for "crossing the center line," the driver must "cause another vehicle to yield." In other states the law reads that it's not a violation if a vehicle merely "bumps" the center line and no other vehicle had to yield the right of way. Therefore, it's important that you look over your state's laws so you'll be right all of the time.

When it comes to citing and charging offenders, we should always reread the pertaining section of law before writing anything down. I know that you've made hundreds of cases and feel comfortable with your affidavits, but it doesn't hurt to go back and look over these laws again. If you want to be a *great* interdiction officer then you need to be a *good* traffic cop. The next time that you're waiting in court for your name to be called, get out your law book and read it! Knowledge is power.

When I used to work interdiction in South Carolina, I kept a CB radio in my car. There was a certain towing company that didn't like the police and often expressed ugly things about cops to its customers and on the CB radio. Then one day I was reading my law book and read that the only time a wrecker service can use its lights is at the scene of an accident. Well, I had to educate a few people to make sure that they knew that they were violating this law. Here's something else to note. The lights on a wrecker in my state had to be red in color, not amber.

Read your law book and become knowledgeable on *all* violations. Once again, knowledge is power.

The last thing that I want to talk about is that you need to know your weights and how it correlates with your state's drug laws. Know what amount of drugs is needed in order to seize a vehicle. Know what amount is needed to indict someone with "trafficking narcotics." In court, you're going to be called to task about your knowledge of drug laws. So once again I want to ask you, "This is your profession, so don't you want to be the best at what you do?"

CHAPTER 4

POSSIBLE CRIMINAL INDICATORS

I've been to a lot of interdiction classes over my career and the instructors always seemed to talk about "indicators of criminal activity." They would say "This is an indicator" and "That's an indicator." The instructors often referred to other ones as well. This frequently left me wondering, *"What makes 'this or that' indicators?"*

Over this chapter, I'll talk about several indicators of possible criminal activity. I'll even go further to explain what the indicators "indicate" and what qualifies as possible criminal indicators.

First of all, I want to clarify that indicators are *not* against the law. They're merely indicators of possible criminal activity. If you come across any of these on your traffic stop, please keep in mind that these are just "possible" indicators of criminal activity. The goal of interdiction is to find several overwhelming criminal indicators that lead to *probable cause*. The more indicators that you see then the better it's for you. Again, I have to emphasize that indicators are not against the law.

I want to give you an example. Let's say that you're working the interstate and you observe an older Ford Bronco drive past you. You notice that the luggage rack on top is wrapped with barbwire. You think of all of the thousands of vehicles that you've seen traveling down the interstate and you've never seen one like this. There just might be a logical explanation for the barbwire, but then again, this might be a possible indicator. Now you need to find a legitimate reason to stop the vehicle so you can begin looking for other possible indicators as well getting a suspicious interview with the driver.

Alarm bells should be going off if the driver has told you that he's driven down from Connecticut to suntan at Daytona Beach and after an hour is heading back home. *The little, dwarf jester from* Game of Thrones *should be jumping up and down in front of your squad car and waving a big, red flag.*

A similar situation like this actually happened to me once except for the barbwire on the luggage rack (and the little, dwarf jester, of course). It turned out to be a good stop. It was a stolen vehicle and the driver was in possession of marijuana.

Business or Pleasure

People are on the road for one of two reasons: business or pleasure.

Let's talk about business first. We're now living in the computer age. We're also going through a recession. People are trying to save as much money as possible. I really doubt if we ever see the day again when businessmen in dark suits, skinny ties, and black fedoras, board an airplane in New York City to fly to Miami for a two hour business meeting and be back home by dinnertime.

Businesses are now using online meeting tools for their conference calls. This is more cost effective and beneficial to the companies. Why waste time and money on travel expenses when you can attend a meeting from the convenience of your home or office?

Business trips should be easy to confirm. They're usually planned in advance. The longer a person waits to book a flight, the higher the price of a plane ticket. It'll cost a businessman at least a thousand dollars or more if he tries to buy a ticket at the airport the day of the flight. It doesn't make good business sense to frivolously waste money like this.

Now I want to talk to you about rental vehicles. Think back and ask yourself if anyone has ever rented you a vehicle since you've become an adult? If so, they were probably with you on your trip. Subsequently, a third party rental should be considered as "suspicious." Why would someone rent a car for a second party and not be present during the trip?

Next, I want to talk to you about GPS (Global Positioning System). There used to be a time that most people (businessmen or vacationers) traveled the interstate carrying MapQuest directions with them. This is no longer true. The modern GPS has replaced MapQuest.

Nowadays, most interstate travelers have a GPS mounted on their windshields. Therefore officers should take a few extra seconds to ask drivers where they're coming from and where they're going. Then they should look closely at the estimated arrival time on the GPS (it should be in *plain view*) to see if it matches up with the distance that they've claimed they've travelled. This is a great reference to see if a suspicious story matches up with the information on the GPS.

Here's something else to note. If you make a roadside seizure from a traffic stop then be sure to get a search warrant for the GPS. The GPS is a great source of information to let you know where the driver is going and where he's been.

Look at the GPS settings! The driver might have even stored some of his favorite addresses in the settings. The GPS is a viable tool that might help you with your investigation.

If you start seeing multiple indicators of criminal activity then don't be intimidated to call the driver's company to verify his trip. This call should be made as you're asking the driver clarifying questions.

If the driver is traveling on business then he should have receipts. Companies keep receipts of their business expenses for tax write-offs. Most companies make their employees pay out of pocket for their business expenses. Then they can turn them in to the company for reimbursement. Therefore, if a person is on a business trip then it would be in his best interest to maintain proper documentation of their trip. This is especially true if the person travels on a weekly basis for his company.

The second reason for being on the roadways is for *pleasure*. With fuel at an all time high, fewer people are joyriding. Consequently, most people just don't get in a car and take a trip without preplanning first. Once again, it's all about saving money. It doesn't matter if it's a business trip or a personal trip. Why waste money?

Here's something else to consider. What do you have if there are two people in a vehicle that live in different states? For example, what if the driver is from New York City and the passenger is from Seattle, Washington? They tell you that they're traveling from New York to Miami, Florida for vacation.

Now, there's no law prohibiting people from doing this, but why would a person drive from Seattle to New York City to meet up with a friend to take a vacation to Florida. Why drive from Washington to New York and then drive down to

Florida? Doesn't it make more sense to fly to Florida from Washington and meet the friend there? Wouldn't this be more cost efficient? Try to estimate the amount of fuel that it'd cost someone to drive from Washington to New York and then to Florida and back to Washington again.

Later in this chapter, we'll further break down business and pleasure trips. We'll put business and pleasure trips in some scenario training to better illustrate criminal activity on the highways and byways.

Driving Behavior

Earlier in the introduction of this book, I vaguely touched on driving behavior. I compared "working interdiction" to being "radar certified." I concluded that you have to get out on the roadways in order to learn driving behavior.

I'll give you as many examples as I can to help get you started. You'll have to learn the rest on your own and perfect it to a craft. Driving behavior *alone* is not *probable cause*. You have to observe a violation in order to stop the vehicle.

When I worked for the state police, I used to set up my interdiction details on an interstate or highway. I'd look for a clear, open area so I could see traffic for about a half mile to a mile. I also wanted to set up on a point where drivers had to notice my position during the flow of traffic. Once I'd established my spot where my marked squad car would be visible to oncoming traffic, I focused all of my attention there. I'd watch for a driver's quick reaction after he saw my squad car.

Did he do something out of the ordinary for no apparent reason? For example, let's say that I observed a vehicle traveling at the 70 mph speed limit. Suddenly it *slows down* to 52 mph (well below the speed limit) after seeing my cruiser. It's as if the driver put down an anchor.

Now let's break this down so I can explain why this behavior is suspicious. Most people, meandering down the interstate, want their piece of pie right out of the middle. If the speed limit is 70 mph then they think they can go 80 mph… right?

I can't even begin to tell you how many times that I've been asked by the general public what leeway cops are willing to allow people to travel over the speed limit before stopping and citing them. I'm sure that you've been asked this question countless times as well. The answer should be *zero* because one mile over the speed limit is against the law.

What I've learned in my career from working interdiction is that *money goes fast* and *dope goes slow.* While working vehicle interdiction, you'll catch a lot of "wanted people" driving slow and overcautiously. For instance, they'll signal 1,000 feet before they have to make the turn.

Here's another example of what's happened to me on several occasions during my career. Once I remember setting up on my "sweet spot" on the interstate and observing a car and a tractor-trailer traveling down the highway. Both vehicles were going the speed limit, but when the driver of the car spotted me, it cut off the tractor-trailer by making a sudden and improper lane change. The car swiftly changed lanes and cut off the truck. Then it slowed down causing the tractor-trailer to change lanes and pass the car. As the truck driver passed by my position, he honked his air horn and gestured at me by throwing up his hands out of frustration. Now I felt obligated to respond to this indiscretion by stopping that car.

Let me ask you this, "Why would someone impulsively change lanes without signaling in full view of a marked police cruiser, cut off a tractor-trailer, and then slow down?" Over the course of a shift, you may see hundreds of cars driving past you and only one driver will behave this way. Not hundreds of drivers…just this one person.

Let's set up another scenario. You've positioned yourself on the highway and you're watching traffic. You observe a lone automobile coming towards you. It slows down as it's traveling in the fast lane. The driver signals his turn way in advance before he changes lanes. This vehicle drives past you and you notice the driver looking back over his shoulder to see if you're coming after him. Then he drives off onto the shoulder of the road. This is one of my favorite driving behaviors that I used to look for and here's why.

First of all, most people slow down when they see a squad car. This is a given. Even off duty cops who are traveling outside their jurisdiction in their personal vehicles behave in this same manner. They immediately start applying pressure to the brake pedal when they see a cop that they don't know.

A lot of people when they see the police will signal their lane changes and try to observe all traffic laws. Then again, why was this person so nervous that he looked over his shoulder to see if you were following him? If the driver wasn't doing anything wrong then why would he look over his shoulder at you? If the driver wasn't doing anything criminal then why is he so nervous? Why did he drive off the roadway?

Other signs of suspicious behavior that I looked for was when everyone in the vehicle began "buckling up" and looking back at me. *Is this suspicious?* I've seen a car drive past me and as I looked the driver right in his eyes, suddenly three other passengers popped up from sleeping and started putting on their seat belts.

Now, let's talk about what's wrong with this picture. Think about the last time that you went on a vacation and you had your family with you. You were several hundred miles into your trip and your family is sleeping while you're driving. What do you do when you spot a highway patrolman, sitting in the middle of the median, watching traffic? Do you drive by -maintaining your speed- and nod to the trooper as if you're saying "hello." Or do you yell at everyone in the car "Hey, it's the cops!"

A law abiding citizen will let his family sleep because he hasn't done anything wrong. Besides it's a gift from your family if you're driving down the road and everyone's asleep but you. This is your "vacation before your vacation." This is the time that you get to have some peace and quiet. You're able to listen to whatever you want to listen to on the radio and think about all of the things that you want to do. This is your time.

The violation to stop this vehicle is "failure to maintain lane of travel." You might not think that this is a big deal… right? The driver just bumped the line… right? However, I want to emphasize that this is a serious violation.

Here's why I'm big on enforcing this violation. Think about all of the times that you've traveled down the highway and noticed the white painted crosses along the throughway. The first step in crashing into a tree is driving off the roadway. Crossing over that line may lead to striking a broken down vehicle as some unfortunate soul is changing a flat tire.

Remember that many of us work for the Department of Public Safety and by stopping this driver then we might've saved his life. We might've prevented an accident further down the road. You also have to think about how many times that you've been on a traffic stop and while speaking with the driver, another vehicle drove by so close to you that you were almost sideswiped.

I lost a good friend, a fellow officer, who was hit and killed by a driver from Pennsylvania. My friend, a state trooper, had pulled his cruiser over behind a broken down vehicle and was helping a stranger change a flat tire. Soon after he was killed, South Carolina legislators changed the law and mandated that vehicles had to slow down or change lanes for stopped emergency vehicles. This is a great ruling and I fully support laws like this one.

Once you've become experienced and start getting this driving behavior down, then it's going to become like second nature. Remember that the majority of your forty hour work week consists of looking out of the front windshield of your patrol vehicle. You have to put in the time to get proficient at seeing this suspicious behavior. And you will! Before long, you'll be riding with someone and you'll ask "Did you see that?" and the untrained officer will have missed it. Therefore practice, practice, practice! You need to practice daily.

You'll need to confirm or deny your suspicions while observing these driving behaviors. Pull out and follow them and get your violations. If you don't get a violation then don't make a traffic stop. Never jeopardize your integrity! You can always give the vehicle's description to someone else working further down the road. Or you can be patient because, more than likely, in the near future, that person will travel down that same road or highway again and you'll be waiting for him.

I know that you've heard this before and you're probably thinking to yourself, *"Yeah right. Sounds good, but this never happens."* It does happen and it happened to me when I was a city officer. I can recall that I kept getting information about a particular drug dealer. I'd seen this person drive past me on multiple occasions, but I had never observed a violation. Then one day the stars must've been aligned in my favor and *karma* caught up with that person. I got him! If this doesn't seem to ever happen to you then remember that there are a lot of bad guys out there so don't be preoccupied with one specific person.

I can still remember the days when I used to go to court and I'd raise my right hand and swear "to tell the truth, the whole truth, so help me God." Whatever I'd say or any other police officer would say was taken to be the "gospel truth." Our testimonies were followed by guilty verdicts. We did a fine job and we were viewed by the public and courts as honorable men who had sworn an oath to tell the truth.

Well, those days are long over. Just like every other profession, we've been beat up on over the years. With new technology such as "dashboard cameras" and "body cameras" almost everything that we do should be on video… right? If it's not on video then it didn't happen… right?

This is not good for us anymore...but this is how it is. We've had to change with the times. We now live in a world where our words and deeds are being recorded and played without our knowledge or consent on the evening news, social media, or the internet.

At this time we *have* to step up our game so we can be better at what we do. We can overcome anything that the courts and public throw our way... and we will. We have to adapt to the changing times just like the famous saying, "There's more than one way to skin a cat."

In this new world of technology, cops need to lock down their probable cause on video as much as they possibly can. For example, let's say that you're sitting on the interstate and see two vehicles coming your way. They're "following too close." Hit the record button on your dash cam so that when they pass your squad car you'll be able to capture the moving violation and probable cause on video.

I started practicing this as soon as I got a camera installed in my patrol vehicle. Think about it, *"What's the first thing that gets challenged at a suppression hearing?"* The answer is "your reason for stopping the vehicle." However, if you have the violation on camera then you're already ahead of the ball game.

When I worked for the state of South Carolina, my agency bought new cameras to put in all of the state police cruisers. Like most government agencies, they went with the lowest bid. These cameras were awful! They were the worse cameras ever, but to bureaucrats who control an agency's purse strings, the lowest bid is *always* the best bid. In all probability, another factor in making this bureaucratic and "political" decision was that the dashboard camera company was also located in South Carolina.

Anyway, this dashboard camera would start recording as soon as I'd key up my radio. It would stop recording whenever I keyed up again. Therefore, this camera would be turned off and on again several times during the course of a normal traffic stop.

I once had a case in Marion County (South Carolina) where I made an arrest on a traffic stop. I had just finished up citing a vehicle and I turned off my rotating lights and dashboard camera. I cleared the radio, but what I didn't know was that when I keyed up to clear the camera, it kicked back on and started recording. So here I am driving down the road, minding my own business, and listening to my favorite radio station (*I'm glad that I wasn't singing out of tune*). This went on for about ten minutes. I think that I might've even made a phone call to check in at home. All of a sudden, as I'm turning into a curve, here it came; a car barrowing around the corner, traveling well over 100 mph. It passed several cars on a double yellow line and caused me to drive off the road to prevent a head on collision.

Low and behold, I got all of this on video. Wouldn't you know it, but the reckless driver was an attorney whom I had gone up against several times. She was very good at her job.

I'll keep this story short. The fine was paid and the judge wanted to know how I got all of this on video. I respectfully responded, "If it's not on video then it didn't happen." I reminded the judge that I had heard this statement being made over and over again in his courtroom.

Consequently, you should practice getting your probable cause on video. This makes your job easier especially when you go to court. Always prepare for every arrest and every citation to go to court.

Here are some more driving behaviors that you'll see on the streets. Look for excessive eye contact in the mirrors. It's suspicious whenever the driver is preoccupied with trying to see where you are in his mirrors. It's also suspicious if you pull up beside a car and all you can see in the driver's side mirror is the entire face of the motorist.

Here's another example. You're behind a vehicle and you notice that the driver in front of you keeps checking the driver's side mirror, then the rear view mirror, then over to the passenger's side mirror. He repeats this behavior every couple of seconds. This should be considered as being very suspicious and here's why.

Think back to when you were in Drivers' Education. The instructor told you that you should check your mirrors often as you're driving… and you should. But here's what I've learned over my career enforcing the laws on the highways and working interdiction. Most of the things that we were taught in Drivers' Education stayed behind in the classroom.

Most people don't drive with their hands on the steering wheel at the "ten and two" position. Most people don't check their mirrors every three seconds.

Can you imagine going on a trip that involves eight hours of driving and checking your mirrors every three seconds? During the first five minutes into your trip you'd have to go get adjusted by your chiropractor. This behavior is just not practiced by licensed drivers. I call this the "Three Second Rule for Mirrors."

Whenever I'd get a violation on a vehicle, I liked pulling up next to the car so I could look inside it. Now, I know what you're probably thinking and we're going to cover this right now. *I don't profile and I never have.* I support legislation against this. Profiling a person to determine if you are going to stop a vehicle is wrong and illegal, so don't ever do this!

Now, let's go back and finish this scenario. I liked to pull up next to a vehicle before making the traffic stop. There're many reasons for doing this. Let me list them for you.

The first reason is so that I can identify a driver just in case the attempted traffic stop leads to a pursuit. If the chase becomes dangerous, (and most of them do) it puts us, as well as the general public, at risk. If you can positively identify the fleeing driver then you can go through the Department of Motor Vehicles and get a photo to match up with whomever you saw driving the getaway vehicle and get an arrest warrant.

I can even make a better suggestion. You should've already activated your dashboard camera since you have a violation and you're going to stop this vehicle. As you pull up next to the offender, take your camera and point it over to the driver and get his face on video. Then move it back before making the traffic stop.

The second reason is that it makes it impossible for a driver and passenger to switch places because you can now identify the driver.

Think back to how many times that you've seen this happen during your career.

The third reason for pulling up next to the vehicle is to see if there are any small children inside the car. If children are present then this should discourage you from getting into a high speed pursuit. The last thing that you want on your conscience is to know that you chased an impulsive parent who had kids inside the car. The worst case scenario that I can imagine is that the fleeing driver crashes his or her car and the children are killed or critically injured. This would be a public relations nightmare and a potentially career-ender for a well intentioned officer.

I want to emphasize again that you should identify the driver and go back later with an arrest warrant and pick that person up. If your state has such a law then be sure to additionally charge him or her with child endangerment.

The fourth reason is to make sure that the driver and passengers are in compliance with the seatbelt law or the cell phone hands-free laws. This could be another violation to stop the vehicle so that you can investigate their suspicious behaviors.

There are several other reasons for pulling up next to the offender's vehicle before stopping it. I could go on for a while. These are just a few highlights. I want to finish this section with something that you and your department should carefully consider such as keeping a Racial Profile Log.

I know what you're thinking, *"Another form to fill out."* We already have so many things that we have to do and document, but a racial profile log is just like a radar log format. What's noted on this form is the reason for the traffic stop, the driver and passengers' age and ethnicity, and what action was taken such as a ticket or verbal or written warning.

I've had a few complaints in my career about racial profiling and the person who complained on me didn't know that I kept these records. The complaint was never sustained and my records were reviewed and no action was ever taken against me. I never worried about these complaints because I've always treated people the same and always will.

I want to talk to you about some other driving behaviors that you'll run across as you're working interdiction. Here's one that you'll see quite a bit in your career. It's called the *"No Look" Look.*

Say that you're parked in the median of a four lane interstate and a motorist drives past you but will not make eye contact or even look your way. It's almost like *"If you don't see me then I don't see you."* There's no law that says people have to look at us or acknowledge our presence. So, let me break this down for you and explain why this behavior is suspicious.

Through my experience, I've learned that the general public is nosy. If you don't agree with me then the next time that you go out to eat at a restaurant, park your patrol car out in front. Go inside and get a seat where you can watch your car.

I'll bet you that almost every time a person walks by your car, they'll look inside it.

Where am I going with this? The majority of people who see a police cruiser parked in the median of an interstate will look at the officer as they drive by. This is a curiosity that's somewhat intrinsic to human behavior. Some people may look at the officer because they might know him. This cop might be an old high school buddy or someone who attends their church or a parent of one of their children's friends. Or they may look at him to see what he's doing.

Therefore, it always seemed suspicious to me if a motorist passed me on the interstate or a back highway and kept looking straight ahead. Driving with his hands in the "ten and two" position on the steering wheel. Once again this behavior is *not* against the law…but it *is* suspicious.

Now let's talk about the "ten and two" driving position. This technique is taught during driver's education and is left behind in the classroom after a person has graduated from the program. There are not too many people driving "ten and two" anymore. Think about the last time that you did all of the driving on a long distance trip. Did you drive with your hands on the steering wheel in the "ten and two" position? Of course not, your arms would've been worn out. A strong majority of people drive with just one hand on the steering wheel.

This is another driving behavior that you can study when working a traffic detail or drug interdiction. Take a mental survey and note driving practices and behaviors. Keep learning about traffic and traffic patterns. Your squad car is your classroom! You can never stop learning.

Motorists who appear to be driving *overly* safe or *overly* cautious fall into this category of what we've just covered. Look for drivers traveling down the highway who suddenly switch into an *overly* safe driving practice whenever they see you. It's also highly suspicious if you see a driver gripping the steering wheel so tight that his knuckles are turning white and his forearms, biceps, and triceps are flexing.

Here are some other suspicious driving behaviors. For example, the driver keeps his right hand on the steering wheel while using his left hand to cover up the left side of his face. Or the driver is looking down at his car radio and acting like he's changing the station. This is suspicious behavior if you observe a motorist heading your way, looking straight ahead, and suddenly he starts messing with the radio.

I've been talking a lot about when people don't look at us. I want to change gears and talk about when they do look at us and how this behavior can be suspicious.

It's suspicious whenever a driver passes by a marked squad unit and gives the "deer in the head lights look" or the expression of *"Oh no!"*

Sometimes you may see a driver muttering something under his breath like *"Oh my god!"* I've become very good at reading lips over the years. I'm not a lip reading expert, but I've had my share of great cases where this has happened.

Then there is *"the Look."* The look that you make after your spouse yells at you for forgetting to take out the trash. The "shocked" look of surprise that you make after you're caught doing something that you shouldn't be doing. This is the very same look on your face that you make whenever you forget important dates in your life.

It's funny that my wife has actually said to me, "How is it that you can see driving behavior a mile down the road, but you can't see that the trash needs to be taken out when it's right in front of you?"

One of my favorites is when a vehicle passes me and the driver is leaning so far back that he's almost in the backseat. The kicker is when he passes me and turns his head around, looking out the back window to see if I'm coming after him. You'd think that the driver leaning that far back had to be eight feet tall, but whenever I stopped him I discovered that he was of normal height.

Another thing that nervous people do when they drive past a police officer is to pick up a cell phone or light up a cigarette. I've found it to be amusing whenever I've observed a car with three people coming towards me and all three put their cell phones up to their ears as they're looking at me.

I once stopped a vehicle for speeding and as I was walking up to the car I noticed that the driver was on his cell phone. I made a passenger side approach and I heard the violator say:

"Dad, I think you're going to have to come get the car."

"He does?" I asked him. "Why does he need to come get the car?"

The expression on this guy's face was priceless. Another case number please!

How about when a driver passes by you and everyone in the car lights up a cigarette. Well here is how you can tell if it is suspicious or not. Look at the cigarettes to see if everyone's are about the same length. If everybody just lit up then the cigarettes should all be the same length. They should've only smoked less than 10 percent of the cigarette. It's as if the traveler in the backseat pulled out three cigarettes and lit up one after another and passed them around as soon as you pulled out after them.

Make sure to look in the ashtray once you've made the traffic stop. See if there's anything inside it before going back to your car to call in their information and write them a citation or a warning. When you come back up to the vehicle, be sure to check this area again. If the ashtray is filled up with nine cigarettes in a short amount of time then you need to start investigating why they're so nervous.

Here are some other things to try to find when working the highway. Look for cars that seem to be carrying a lot of weight in the trunk area. See if the rear tires are heavily weighed down under a hefty load or the rear of the vehicle looks as if it's about to drag to the ground.

A single key on a key ring could be another indicator of illegal activity. Most people put their house keys and work keys on the same key ring.

Then what makes a single ignition key on a key ring an indicator? A drug smuggler may pick up a transport vehicle from a drug trafficking organization and they'll give him a single key to the ignition.

Why? If the smuggler is caught then the other keys on a key ring that belong to another person may tie that smuggler to other members of a criminal organization. This is why they remove all keys but one.

Keep this in mind whenever you're working an undercover detail and you pick up an unmarked detail car (usually a confiscated vehicle from a drug arrest) from your fleet. Prostitutes and other members of the criminal underworld have learned to look inside vehicles to see if the interior is clean and if there's a single key in the ignition. They know that if there's only one key then there's a good chance that they're talking to a cop. Therefore after picking up an undercover car to work a drug sting or a prostitution detail, be sure to dirty up the interior of the car and remember to put other keys on the key ring (remove your handcuff key) so they can be seen hanging from the ignition. Just as cops get better with each arrest, so do the criminals after they've been arrested. They talk to each other and share information too.

Forced entry into a automobile could mean a couple of different things. On most stolen vehicles you'll discover that the little window on the drivers' side rear door has been knocked out. Guess which is also the most expensive window to replace? Yes, it's the smaller one. I guess someone wanting to make money did their homework.

The keyhole on a trunk or a driver's door is another one. Criminals are getting better at hiding their forced entry. It's called "bumping" and they're using a tennis ball to help pop the lock to get inside.

Window tint is something else that you might want to consider. Know your state's laws and how darkly tinted car windows can be. Smugglers who travel great distances aren't familiar with all of the states' laws on window tinting, so they'll tint all of

their windows except for the front windshield. They want to limit any negative encounters with law enforcement. There's also a famous saying in law enforcement that goes, *"Evil seeks darkness."*

Just saying!

Another criminal indicator might be when a motorist travels down the highway with all four windows rolled down. Why is this suspicious? A drug mule might've seen you sitting in the median of the interstate and he knows that he has violated the window tint law. So, he rolled down all four windows to take away your reason for stopping him. What's even more suspicious is when the driver does this in cold weather.

Let's cover again why this is suspicious behavior. Think back to when you were driving a vehicle and a passenger in the backseat rolled down the back window. What happened? The pressure from the opened window hurt your ears. This fluttering feeling in your eardrums is a miserable way to travel. Usually someone in the car yells at that person to roll the window up.

Let's cover another example. Say that you see a minivan traveling down the highway with only one person inside. You noticed that the back windows were cracked open about an inch and it's in the middle of wintertime. It's also 15 degrees outside.

Why would a person do this when it's freezing outdoors? What I've learned over the years is that when a person's hauling illegal goods, he'll crack the back windows to vent out the smell of contraband. It's as if the driver is paranoid about the odor.

Now a logical explanation could be that the motorist is smoking cigarettes and venting through the back windows to regulate the temperature inside his car. So I can understand that he has a valid reason to vent out through these back windows. This is why none of these indicators *alone* mean anything in a court of law unless you have other indicators to go along with them.

A single tire that's heavily weighted down can give you a reason to believe that you might have a "tire load." A drug smuggler can actually travel easily down the road on a loaded tire filled with contraband. Most of the time, drug mules have to get these "loaded" tires balanced or it'll beat them up on the road. Most tires will have at least one or two weights to help balance the tire. However, you'll probably need to investigate a driver who's operating a vehicle with a tire that has six weights or more. Dope, in a loaded tire, is usually hidden in a collar located inside the tire.

Dealer Stickers and Bumper Stickers

I used to take my time whenever I'd walk up to a car so I could "read it." Here's my advice, take your time to read dealer stickers and bumper stickers. For instance, if I stopped a car that had a dealer sticker from West Palm Beach, Florida, I'd ask the driver how long he'd owned the vehicle. If he said it was "brand new" then he should know where he'd bought it (This is just a conversation piece). Even if the driver purchased a used car, you should know that most used car dealerships will place franchise decals on the bumper or a front license plate to advertise their businesses.

Bumper stickers are one of my favorite things that tell me about the people inside the vehicle. While working interdiction, I began noticing a pattern with bumper stickers. I'm going to list my favorite stickers and then talk about each one. Look for bumper stickers about car insurance, American flags, religious references and icons, law enforcement, military, "Say No to Drugs," "DARE," "MADD," "My Kid's an Honor Roll Student," and "I Love my Wife!"

Stickers are just what they are…stickers. People will express themselves in many different ways with bumper stickers. They'll show support for the things that they like. This may be religious, political, hobbies, sports related, or even a local high school team.

Through my experience and what I've found to be consistent with my arrests are the following bumper stickers. Keep in mind that this is not 100 percent, but merely my personal experience while working the road. I want to remind you that bumper stickers *alone* are not probable cause or a reason to stop anyone. However, I've gone back and looked over my past cases and at the pictures of the vehicles that I've seized and I've noticed a pattern. Again, this is just my personal research that I've done during my career.

There's nothing wrong with being religious and this is not against the law. However, when you start noticing an overabundance of anything you might want to start elevating your suspicion that something's not right with this situation or this person.

For example, say that you've stopped a car and you notice thirteen pairs of rosary beads hanging from the rearview mirror. You see six pictures of Catholic saints inside the interior, but the first thing out of the driver's mouth is "How long is this going to (effing) take?" Then he dropped a string of f-bombs long enough to make a longshoreman blush.

To me, this is not consistent with a person who takes his relationship with God seriously. My father-in-law is a Baptist minister and I'm sure that he doesn't talk this way when he's teaching a Bible study or visiting the shut-ins.

To further break this down, I want to explain why this could possibly be an indicator or an item of interest. Catholics may carry a single pair of rosary beads with them throughout their entire life. Thirteen pairs of rosary beads may be an indication of guilt. They're overcompensating for something that they've done wrong or are currently doing wrong.

I once stopped a motorist and when he got out of the car he had a Bible in his hand. This person also was tapping his heart with his right hand and looking up towards the sky and he was praying.

Immediately I knew that something wasn't right. After I got his license, I went back to run the information through my computer. I continued to watch him as he began acting more strangely. He kept striking his chest as he was sitting on the bumper. Then he started standing up quickly and sitting back down again. He did this about fourteen times, all in less than five minutes. He was making facial grimaces as if he'd been stung by a swarm of hornets. It didn't take long for me to find out that he had several active warrants and he was wanted by the US Marshals.

My favorite bumper stickers are the ones that read, "Say No to Drugs!" Here's the irony. From my experience, I've usually found contraband inside the cars that I've stopped with these bumper stickers. I've talked to many other interdiction cops who've told me the same thing.

The same goes for bumper stickers that read "MADD" (Mothers Against Drunk Drivers). I cannot begin to tell you how many times that I've found open containers inside these vehicles.

Law enforcement stickers are others that I liked seeing. It's as if the people buying these stickers to publicly show their support for law enforcement are *really* masking what they're *really* doing. They don't want law enforcement stopping them.

Most cops that I know won't put police stickers on their personal vehicles. Most cops don't want the general public on the roadways to know that they work in law enforcement. It puts them in the public's crosshairs. Besides, if you've ever stopped an off-duty officer you'll know right away that they're in law enforcement.

It's not illegal to have several law enforcement stickers on your vehicle, but if you see thirteen FOP (Fraternal Order of Police) stickers on one car then it might be suspicious. Why is this person working so hard to convince you that he or she supports their local FOP lodge?

State law mandates that everyone driving on the road must have car insurance. This is required so that innocent parties are covered in case of an accident. Consequently, whenever I'd see a vehicle with four stickers on the bumper that read "State Farm" or "Allstate Insurance," I'd get suspicious. Once again, what I've learned from my experience is that the driver isn't insured. This has been consistent with what I've seen over my career.

The American flag is something that proud Americans often display on their vehicles. These car owners may have been former veterans or may have family members serving overseas. There's nothing wrong with displaying your support for this great country.

I'm proud that I served my country when I joined the United States Navy. In all of my travels teaching schools, I've always surveyed my students and asked how many had served in the United States military. I'd ask those who raised their hands, "How many American flags do you have on your personal vehicles?" Ninety-five percent of those surveyed would answer "Zero!" These are officers who are proud to have served their country. They're highly patriotic -no matter who's in the White House- but they don't feel the need to display six American flags on their vehicles.

So, whenever I'd see a vehicle traveling on the highway displaying ten flags, I'd get suspicious. What I've discovered is that the person driving is often an illegal alien. They're *over-compensating* their support for this country. They're hoping to be accepted whenever they're really here illegally.

Another bumper sticker that I was used to seeing read, "I Love My Wife." I've often found these stickers on pickup trucks parked after hours in city parks with another vehicle pulled up beside it. Oftentimes, I'd pull up behind these vehicles so I could investigate what they're doing in the park after it was closed. What I've discovered was that the person in the pickup truck was not the driver's wife.

It's almost as if when any of these bumper stickers are displayed on vehicles they really mean the exact opposite. I want to stress again that bumper stickers *alone* do not create enough probable cause to make a traffic stop. These examples are just my personal observations that I've made throughout my career. There are many more bumper stickers out there that you'll soon discover to be consistent with what we've already covered.

Fast Food Litter

When my wife and I used to travel the interstates across the country teaching our seminars, we'd often stop to eat at fast food restaurants. We'd go through the drive-through window so we didn't waste much time. We're not much different than other travelers who have to be somewhere by a certain time. Many busy people eat on the road. However, most people throw away their trash at the next stop.

What I've found to be suspicious is discovering several days of fast food wrappers inside an automobile on a traffic stop. What this means to me is that the driver didn't want to stray too far away from his vehicle. Drug traffickers hauling contraband are held accountable by the criminal organizations.

They're in big trouble if the drug stash gets "ripped off." They're now responsible to pay back whatever is lost with their own lives or they have to pay off the debt by smuggling more drugs without reimbursement. This explains why a car may appear to be lived in during a three-day trip.

These Mexican drug cartels don't have a "sense of honor" like it was in earlier days with the Italian Mafia. The Mafia left families alone. However, with violence spilling across our southern borders from Mexico, these drug mules know that if they mess up and lose the stash then the cartels will kill their families. This is another reason why they don't let the car out of their sight.

Airline and Bus Tickets

I also liked finding airline or bus tickets inside a vehicle while searching it. This helped me break down the driver's recent travel plans. It's like putting together a puzzle except I'm using their travel itinerary and receipts as the pieces.

For instance, you may find out on a random traffic stop that the passenger left on a bus the same day that the driver left for his destination. You may discover by examining the receipts that both people left Miami, Florida on Monday and were heading to New York City. The driver and passenger (who took the bus) both arrived close to the same time on Tuesday. Then you discover that on Wednesday, they shared a car ride back from New York City to Miami. What a strange coincidence. You can apply this same logic to airline tickets.

Maps

Look for maps inside the vehicle. Fewer people are using maps these days. We're living in the "computer age" and most people are using a GPS or their cell phones for directions. Nonetheless, you should examine these maps closely and see if you can tell if the maps came from rest areas. Someone traveling to Florida for pleasure, such as vacationers, will pick up these maps for the advertisements of what's in an area such as the Kennedy Space Center.

Air Fresheners

In the world of interdiction, air fresheners have always been considered as "suspicious." Some cars with air fresheners can be completely innocent such as a family that wants to get the dog stench out of their car or the disgusting odor of their kids' smelly feet and stale potato chip farts, but what I liked looking for was an *overwhelming* amount of air fresheners. *This was suspicious!*

It would be in your best interest to investigate a vehicle if you can smell a strong aroma of air fresheners ten feet away before you even make contact with the driver.

Let me explain why multiple air fresheners are suspicious. How can a sane person drive 20 hours inside a car while having to smell the overwhelming pungent odor of ten to fifteen air fresheners without going crazy?

It's suspicious if you have a headache from the powerful pungency of pine scented air fresheners within the first minute of collecting the driver's information. This will not occur if the driver only has a couple of pine tree air fresheners.

There's a big difference in having one air freshener or sixteen air fresheners inside a vehicle. The same goes for keeping a box of dryer sheets in the back window. The purpose for this is that the sun will heat up the drier sheets and scent the car.

Cologne and Perfume

A strong aroma of cologne or perfume is something else to reconsider. It's suspicious if you make a car stop and notice that the driver just sprayed cologne several times inside his vehicle. Again, you must ask yourself, "Why would anyone do this?"

Another indicator of suspicious behavior is someone who personalizes a rental vehicle. Why would anyone put stickers or install a CB (citizens band radio) on a vehicle that has been rented for two days? Look at the key ring and see if the driver has personalized it. Is he trying to "disguise" the rental car as his personal vehicle?

U-Haul Trucks

Next, let's talk about U-Haul trucks. What I've found to be suspicious is whenever I located a radar detector inside one of these vehicles. Think back to a time when you might've rented one of these vehicles to move your household goods.

Do you remember loading down the U-Haul with all of your furniture and heading to your new residence? Did you really need a radar detector? You're doing well if you can get one of these trucks to accelerate to 60 mph. Also, ask yourself, "Did you ever install a CB radio when you moved in one of these vehicles?" Then why would it be any different for anyone else? It's not!

Indicators of Methamphetamines

These following items have been consistent with methamphetamine cases. These are the things that I've seen whenever I made "meth" cases.

Toothpicks

One of the indicators of methamphetamine activity is when a driver keeps toothpicks above the visor of his car. *Tweekers* dip toothpicks into baggies of meth and suck on them. When they're done, they stick them above the visor. Whenever they want another meth high, they'll get another toothpick and repeat this process again.

I don't understand why a meth user, with only one tooth in his head, will neglect his personal hygiene, but won't reuse the same toothpick.

High Energy Drinks

Red Alert Mountain Dew cans and high energy drinks are other signs of meth use. Think about the times that you've stopped a car and talked to the driver. You found out that he was on a two day trip. You stopped him six hours into the journey and he's already drank four Red Bull high energy drinks as well as several highly caffeinated Mountain Dews.

The majority of people wouldn't drink more than two energy drinks in a twenty-four hour period. But this person has drunk four high energy drinks and four soft drinks in a period of six hours. You also learn that the driver is unemployed and not in school. *Suspicious?*

Several Pair of Sunglasses

Say that you've stopped a vehicle and you notice that the driver has several pairs of sunglasses inside the car. Sunlight hurts the eyes of people under the influence of methamphetamines. This explains the wraparound sunglasses and five other pairs of shades that you might see inside a car.

Colorful Interior Lights

Another dead giveaway is finding a car at nighttime with illuminated red, orange, or purple interior lights. Why? Oncoming traffic headlights also hurt the meth abuser's eyes. Driving with a colored interior light that's turned on inside the car will help distort oncoming traffic lights.

Latex Gloves

Now I want to talk about medical style latex gloves. Unless the driver and passengers are in the medical profession then why are they carrying latex gloves? Most people don't travel with latex gloves unless they're diabetic, a cop, or a paramedic.

If you have any questions then you should ask the driver directly why he's carrying latex gloves. He may have a good reason. If it's legitimate then it's better to know why back at the car stop then find out the answer later in court.

Unusually Clean Vehicles

These are just a few things that I've noticed over my career that are associated with meth cases. Another sign of methamphetamine use is having a very clean car. People high on meth experience euphoria, high energy, and insomnia. So they'll spend hours shining and polishing their cars and trucks.

They have to do something because they can't sleep. Therefore, you'll find cleaning kits with a variety of cleaning solutions inside these vehicles. I call this the "meth cleaning bucket."

Urine Filled Bottles

It's not that unusual for people to pee in bottles during long trips. I've often polled my classes to see how many students will admit to doing this. I've noticed that the number is always high for males. However, each person said that he disposed of the urine filled bottle at the next stop.

Therefore, if you stop a vehicle and notice seven or eight urine filled bottles in the backseat of a vehicle then you should consider this as very suspicious. What this tells me is that the person didn't have time to stop because the vehicle had to be at a certain destination by a certain time.

This could also mean that the driver has used meth in the past and he's saving his urine to extract out the meth residue and reuse it later. This is called the "Nazi Method." It's impossible for the human body to break down all of the methamphetamine. A *tweeker* can get high on the methamphetamine a second time if he saves his urine. I once came across twenty-seven bottles of urine inside a tractor-trailer…and yes…this was a methamphetamine case.

Two Way Radios

Two-way radios used to be popular in the late eighties and early nineties. However, they're still being used today by people traveling on trips. Thus, keep this in mind, when you see one radio in a car, there's probably a second vehicle traveling with it. If I was searching a vehicle and came across a radio, I liked turning it on and listening to see if anyone else was transmitting. Sometimes, I'd get on the radio and say, "Okay, we're moving!" I'd do this to see if someone else was traveling with them.

I have to caution you to be careful. Know what your state laws will allow you to do and what you can't do. Keep in mind that some of these newer radios are voice activated when they're turned on. You might be unaware that you're transmitting and the other vehicle is listening to everything that you're saying and doing.

Cell Phones

The same thing goes for cell phones that have an automatic answering feature. Some cartel members in an "escort vehicle" traveling with a "load vehicle" will call the drug mule's phone. The phone will be on silent so the officer won't hear it ring, but the person on the other end can listen to the entire conversation without anyone having to answer the phone.

I want to talk about how cell phones can be suspicious. However, let's first talk about what's normal. A lot of people, including cops, have two cell phones: a personal cell phone and a work cell phone.

How this becomes suspicious is the number of contacts on each phone. I always poll my classes and ask the students, "How many contacts do you have stored on your cell phone?" The average number of contacts in a phone is around seventy-five.

What is considered as suspicious is if a driver has three cell phones but only five contacts on each one. You need to examine the phones to see how each contact is listed: first name, last name, or nickname. What is suspicious is a driver that has three cell phones with five contacts or less on each one. This does not seem normal to me.

Boost Phones

Boost phones are also known as "throwaway" phones. For a long time, they were not traceable. Law enforcement had a hard time tracking down these phones. These phones are not against the law but when faced with doubtful circumstances and you find a boost phone then you might want to elevate the investigation.

Final Thoughts

Whenever you've stopped someone and you're in a place where you have a lawful authority to be then take the time to properly scan the vehicle. You're looking for packing materials such as duct tape, food saver bags, and any equipment that can be used to package contraband. Also look for worn screws and mismatched screws. Look for missing screws if you have a new vehicle.

If you do any kind of undercover work then you need to know what an RF Detector is. They're often used by drug trafficking organizations to see if the person they're selling contraband to is wearing a wire. You can go to your local auto shops to see all of the items that they're selling. I strongly suggest that you go to these places and look at all of the aftermarket items for sale. These are what the bad guys are buying to use against you.

Tweety Bird has long been associated with drug trafficking. The "magical thinking" behind this phenomenon is that the drug mules believe that they won't get caught hauling contraband. Think about it. How many times have you watched this cartoon? Did Tweety bird ever get caught?

I'm not saying that if your kids are at home playing with Tweety Bird then they're doing something wrong. Again, when faced with other suspicious behaviors and circumstances, this is just another indicator or an item of interest.

CHAPTER 5

RENTAL VEHICLES

Every day in this country millions of people rent vehicles. Not everyone who rents a car is guilty of doing anything wrong. Out of all of the people who rent vehicles daily only a small percentage are bad apples.

Cops have known for a long, long time that drug smugglers like using rental cars in case they're apprehended by law enforcement. Cops can't seize rental vehicles. If they use their own cars, they're putting their personal vehicles at risk of being confiscated.

Rental vehicles are the perfect automobiles to transport narcotics. These cars are less than two years old and are reliable to get the driver to where he needs to go.

Smugglers also know that their private vehicles are being documented every time they cross the Canadian and Mexican borders. However, their personal tags won't be read by the new technology of License Plate Readers (LPR) if they're traveling in rental cars. One of the great advantages of LPRs is that law enforcement can network and track wherever a suspected vehicle has traveled. The data is stored and can be accessed later in an investigation.

The convenience of renting cars allows smugglers to use a certain car once and then a different car the next time. This makes it even more difficult for law enforcement to track down drug smugglers. This is another reason why third party rentals should be considered as suspicious. The bad guys are using other people's names so there won't be a record of theirs.

Here are some ways to check if a rental vehicle is being used for criminal activity. Closely examine the rental contract to see if it matches up with the driver's story.

Does it make sense?

Check the rental date and return date to see if there was enough time for the driver to make it to the destination and back again.

Check the mileage to see if what the driver has told you lines up with the amount of miles that he claims that he's driven. For example, let's say that you stopped a car and the driver rented a vehicle to drive from Miami to Jacksonville, Florida. He's on his way back to Miami, but has only driven 75 miles.

Say that you make another traffic stop and the driver told you that he was driving from Miami, Florida to New York City. You look at his miles and notice that he's only driven 600 miles. I'd consider both of these scenarios as "suspicious."

Another thing that you should investigate is whether or not the driver of the rental vehicle is the one who actually rented it. This is called a "third-party rental" whenever the person who rented the vehicle is not present on the trip. If the driver of the rental car starts giving you a hard time then you can always call the car rental company and let them know that the driver who's in possession of the vehicle is not on the contract. Oftentimes, the company will give you permission to tow the vehicle to their nearest car rental agency. Study your state's law on this topic so that you'll know what you can legally do and what you can't do. This is another good question to ask your local prosecutor. You can also research the case law pertaining to rental vehicles.

It's suspicious if the driver of the rental vehicle does not have the rental agreement with him. You'll need to challenge him on this and call the local rental company to find out who actually has rented the vehicle.

Normally when a person rents a car, he picks up the paperwork from the counter and walks to the vehicle to check it for damage. At most major airports, the majority of agencies require their customers to show identification and the rental agreement to the attendant at the security booth before leaving the car lot. Therefore, it doesn't make any sense for the driver not to be carrying the car rental agreement inside the rental vehicle. It's almost as if he should pin the rental agreement to his shirt before he even leaves the car lot.

Here are some things that I liked looking for whenever I stopped a rental vehicle. I tried to find out the origin of the rental and the driver's destination. This should always be in your assessment whenever you make any traffic stop.

I liked to read the rental agreement to see if the vehicle was prohibited from leaving the state. For instance, when I worked in South Carolina I discovered that many Florida car rental agencies only allowed their cars to be driven "in state only." If I ever had any issues with the driver, I'd make a courtesy phone call to the rental company. The phone number is always on the agreement and usually the agent who checks out the vehicle writes his or her name on the contract in real big letters such as "Call BECKY." This is a gift that keeps on giving all year long.

I want you to think back to the last time that you rented a vehicle. *Did you ever check the oil or even lift up the hood?* No! We take it for granted that the rental company has provided us with a dependable vehicle. They should've already made sure that everything's in order. I've never checked the oil on any rental car, and I've rented hundreds of vehicles over the years.

Another thing that I've never done is change a flat tire on a rental car. I guess the mindset behind this is that if a tire goes flat then you should call the rental agency and they'll bring you a new vehicle. Some rental companies don't even put spare tires in the trunks of their cars.

Smugglers also know that rental vehicles are not flashy and fit in well with traffic. However, rental cars are very easy to spot. They're newer vehicles -less than two years old- and are almost always clean. The first thing that a rental company does after a car has been returned is to vacuum it and wash it. Rental companies also put barcodes on their vehicles.

A lot of these companies have bumper stickers with their agency's name on them. For example, the Triangle Rent A Car has a big yellow sticker on the rear bumper. Or you'll see the emblem of the company, like a lowercase letter "e" for Enterprise Rent-A-Car.

Of course, whenever you stop a car for a violation and you make a passenger side approach, look at the keychain in the ignition and you should be able to see the company's name on it.

I've had great success with rental cars and trucks over my career. However, it doesn't mean that you have a drug case just because you've stopped a rental car. Again, millions of people rent cars every day, for business and pleasure, and they're not doing anything wrong.

I want to finish this chapter with a story. I'm as pro-law enforcement as a person can get. I've dedicated my entire life to doing this job. I don't want to do anything else in this world.

I've probably rented several thousand cars as I've taught our 420 classes all over this great country of ours. We use these cars on our "search days" to teach officers how to properly search a vehicle.

There have been close to a hundred times that our instructors have found marijuana, crack, heroin, methamphetamines, pills, even a guitar, and much more. We rented these cars and drove them to the 420 schools. It's scary to think that if we would've been stopped; our careers could've been over.

Since then, I've changed my stance on rental vehicles. We shouldn't be searching vehicles just to be searching. We should have overwhelming indicators before searching a vehicle for contraband.

I want to leave it at this. If you stop a rental car and find drugs then you had better make darn sure that it belongs to the person that you're going to charge with "possession of narcotics." You'll have to build your case and go into a court of law. You don't ever want to accuse an innocent person. So, if you find drugs inside a rental vehicle and it's down behind the dash and it looks as if it had been lost or has been there for a while, then I'd do a "found property report."

Then again, if you're seeing indicators, getting a suspicious story, and things don't seem right, then I'm sure that you're on the right path. All I'm saying is this, *"Wow! I can't believe what I just found."* Now place yourself in the driver's shoes and think back to whenever you rented a car. Did you check the car before you left the parking lot?

Here's the last thing that I want to discuss for this chapter. I also stay in a lot of hotel rooms. I like to think that I've stayed in some of the nicer places when traveling. But then again, here's something that actually happened to me. I once found some pills on the floor under the bed of a hotel room.

I have two dogs that I love more than anything. That scared my wife and me to death. As a general practice, we now search our hotel rooms and comb the floors looking for narcotics. Please do the same thing especially if you have little kids crawling on the floor or pets that stay with you. I just recently stayed in a well-known hotel chain in Montana and found meth in a bowl beneath my bed. I went down to the lobby and chewed them out. I could've lost my dogs. I got a free room for the night, but so what. I could've lost my two best friends.

Please be careful in your travels.

CHAPTER 6

TRAFFIC STOP CONSIDERATIONS

We've all made tons of traffic stops over our careers. There are police academies that teach a certain way to make a vehicle stop and other academies teach a different way. It seems that part of a cop's inherent nature is to think that his technique is the "best" and "safest" way to stop a car. Maybe he's right and maybe he's wrong, but no matter how good we are at doing certain things, we can always improve our techniques.

I'm not claiming to be the best that there is at teaching traffic stops, neither am I saying that my way is the only way. You were trained by police academy instructors and veteran officers and by now you should have a feel for what works best for you.

I know what has kept me safe over the years. I've also been assaulted on a roadside traffic stop, so I want to share my experiences with you so that you might learn from me since I had to learn the hard way.

"Officer Safety" should always be our number one priority. I've been to more than enough cop funerals over my career. I've even delivered a Medal of Honor and a death benefits check to an officer's widow. That was one of the toughest things that I've ever done. When do you stop hugging that person whose husband was just killed in the line of duty? What do you say to the weeping children and the grieving mother and father?

I want to make a few proposals in this chapter that might help refine your car stop techniques. It's possible that these personal suggestions could even save your life. By no means am I suggesting that my methods override your department's policies and procedures. What might've worked for me might not work for you.

The first thing that I liked doing was to get my probable cause captured on video. Next, I liked catching up to the violator's vehicle before I ever activated my lights and called in the tag. After I pulled up next to the vehicle, I'd look over at the driver so I could identify him. I was also looking for other driving behaviors and to see if the driver and passengers were complying with the seatbelt law.

Finally, I'd stop the vehicle. Once it's stopped, I'd turn my front wheels out towards traffic in case another vehicle crashed into the back of my car. This way my cruiser would be knocked away from me and any people standing outside the vehicle. This technique was just one more thing that I'd do to protect myself. Remember that you're also responsible for any driver and passengers that you have step outside the car. Therefore, as soon as I'd stop a vehicle, I'd get out of my cruiser and be prepared for almost anything.

I'd always try to approach the driver on the passenger's side. I believe that walking up on the passenger's side of a vehicle is much safer. I didn't like approaching a car on the driver's side where traffic was whizzing by me. Too many drivers are distracted by the whirling emergency lights and fail to see the officer. Besides, I've found it very difficult to hear a driver while interviewing him on the driver's side.

You have a better view of what's inside the car if you're standing on the passenger's side. You're also closer to the glove box after it's been opened up to retrieve the registration and insurance information. The driver is also off balance as he's leaning over the seat and reaching into the glove box. This gives you the tactical edge!

I once stopped a twenty-year-old kid in Darlington County, South Carolina. I immediately noticed that he was acting suspicious as I approached his vehicle on the passenger's side. I asked him for his registration and when he started to reach over to the glove box, he stopped in midair and said, "I don't have it officer."

I told the driver that I wasn't in a hurry and he could take his time to look for all of his documentation. I told him to go ahead and open up the glove box and look for it. I said that I didn't want to issue him a ticket for not having his registration. He was a college kid and I knew that students don't have much money. I really didn't want to issue him a registration ticket. The driver started to reach over to the glove box again and stopped in midair.

"I...I...I... don't have it officer," he repeated a second time. "I'm just going to have to take this ticket."

Once again, I found this to be very suspicious. Here's a twenty-year-old kid in school and he'd would rather take a ticket then look for his registration? I had him step away from his car to talk to me. I asked him why he didn't want to look inside his glove box.

"Is there something in the glove box that you don't want me to see," I asked.

"Yes."

"What's in there?"

"A gun."

I informed the driver that he wasn't legally of age to carry a firearm and I asked him, "Who does it belong to?"

"My dad," he said. "You can take it out of the glove box."

When I removed the pistol from the glove box, I found a checkbook with his pop's name on the checks. There was also a South Carolina driver's license number on the check. I went back to my cruiser so I could run the firearm through NCIC to see if it had been stolen. I also wanted to run his father's license through the system to check for any active warrants. I learned that his father was a convicted felon and was *prohibited* by law from owning or possessing any firearms.

I also noticed that his dad's phone number was on the check. I called him and asked if his son owned a gun? He answered "no" and confirmed that the gun was his and not his son's. I asked him to describe the gun. He told me the make, model, and caliber. He even told me the color. It was an exact match.

I told the father that I didn't want to charge his son for having a weapon in his possession and asked if he'd mind coming down to my traffic stop to meet me. I also asked if he'd write a statement declaring that the gun belonged to him and describe the weapon just as he'd done for me on the phone. I asked him to claim ownership of the weapon so his son wouldn't get into trouble.

The father lived in Lakeview, South Carolina. He drove forty-one miles to meet me and, unbeknownst to him, the ATF agent (whom I had just called). I told the ATF agent that a convicted felon had violated his parole. He was going to show up at my traffic stop and write a statement claiming ownership of the gun.

Here was this guy, a convicted felon, not following the law, sitting on a couch at home when I called. Needless to say this career criminal, who illegally owned a gun and irresponsibly left it inside a car (or lent it to his underage son), had no idea that he was getting ready to go back to prison. After he showed up and wrote a statement claiming ownership, I turned the matter over to the ATF agent who was listening in the backseat of my squad car. He was charged under Project CeaseFire[1] and went back to prison.

The people that you stop are always expecting you to come up on the driver's side. Most people are right-handed and if you approach on the passenger's side, if there are any passengers then they're going to be in harm's way if the driver shoots at you.

One of the disadvantages of standing on the driver's side is that not only do you have to worry

---

[1] Project CeaseFire is the District of South Carolina's implementation of the Department of Justice's Project Safe Neighborhoods (PSN) initiative, which was first unveiled by President Bush and Attorney General Ashcroft in May 2001. PSN is a nationwide commitment to reduce gun crime and make our communities safer.

about being shot by the driver, but you may have to dodge passing traffic. More police officers are killed in the line of duty in automobile accidents or hit by passing vehicles on traffic stops then die from felonious assaults.

There are too many opportunities for a car to strike you while making a driver's side approach. These vehicles are traveling at 70 mph or faster and again, there's too much risk with little to no reward.

Passenger's Side View vs. Driver's Side

Which side has a better view? Think about it! When you walk up on the driver's side and look into the vehicle, most of the driver's body is covering up what's inside the car. What was left open is now covered up as the driver leans forward and reaches into his wallet. You can't see anything inside the car and you can't watch the hands of the driver or passengers.

By going up on the passenger's side, you can see the driver and the entire view of the vehicle's interior is now opened. You can watch the driver's hands and all of his movements. You're able to look at the ignition switch, floorboards, and what's in the passenger seat and the glove box. If the car's stolen, you can look at the steering column to determine if it's been tampered with.

Here's another advantage to making a passenger's side approach. If you're assaulted or get into a physical altercation, then you'll be closer to cover and you won't be as likely to be hit by a passing motorist or an oversized vehicle.

How many times do you see trucks with wide loads traveling down the interstate or back highways? These vehicles are sixteen-feet wide and nearly take up both lanes of traffic.

What we do is never routine. Any traffic stop is potentially dangerous. Therefore, I tried to go above and beyond to make sure that I stayed safe. For example, whenever possible, I liked putting all four of my tires in the grass. Even more, I liked removing myself and the violator to a safer place if I ever felt that the current location was dangerous. I don't think that anyone would argue with you or judge you for wanting to be safe.

I also preferred to remove the driver from his car and bring him back to the right side of my patrol vehicle. I never stood in the middle of both vehicles. This is called the "Kill Zone." Again, you're responsible for any person that you get out of a vehicle.

On every stop, I'd be as courteous as I possibly could be, no matter what the person had done. Never let your emotions get in the way of your good judgment! This driver just might be a potential juror member on your next big bust. I tried to be as consistent as possible with every stop that I made.

I didn't like working areas that had guardrails…but if you ever do make a car stop along a guardrail, then walk up on the other side of the guardrail. Once you've gathered all of the information, you'll need to walk back to your car on the other side of the guardrail.

Guardrails are not an ideal place to work or make car stops. This is why we covered "preplanning" in the Pre-Patrol Preparations chapter. It's important that you select a good and *safe* place to work your interdiction car stops. You should always try to work in an area that best fits you. Again, I liked working just out on the edge of town. This allowed me to be less than five minutes away from everything.

A driver has no legitimate expectation of privacy of what's in the car's interior if it can be viewed from outside by either an inquisitive spectator or a diligent police officer. Also, odors fall under the "plain view" doctrine on traffic stops.

Here's a little tip. If a driver is smoking his medical marijuana, he has probably already cracked open his window on the driver-side as soon as you pull him over. Subsequently, if you make a passenger's side approach, the wind will blow the smoke back towards you where you can detect the scent.

Officers must have what the courts refer to as an "experienced nose." They must articulate that they had previous knowledge that they knew what marijuana, crack-cocaine, and other drugs smell like.

Here are some warning signs that you need to be aware of when stopping vehicles. Watch what the driver does before you pull him over. See if the driver parks his car on the white line so that if you walk up on the driver's side then you'll be in the lane of traffic.

Has the driver failed to turn off his turn signal after he's been stopped? Is he so nervous that he forgot to turn off the turn signal? This could be a possible danger sign.

A drug smuggler may believe that you're on to him, so he'll turn on his emergency flashers to alert the decoy vehicle traveling with him that you're suspicious of criminal activity. This is a call for help! You should be aware of what's going on around you. This is also known as "felony flashers."

Another warning sign is if it seems to take the driver an exceptional long time to pull over. The driver may be taking a few extra seconds to conceal contraband or make a beacon phone call to his felonious cohorts. It might be that the driver is reaching for a concealed weapon. It could also mean that the driver and passenger are getting ready to switch positions.

Now, I didn't used to get too upset whenever a driver used the turn signal before pulling over on the shoulder of a highway. It didn't bother me that the motorist continued driving a little further down the road to find a safer place to park. He may have been looking for an area of the road that had wider shoulders or no guardrails.

Therefore, keep this in mind whenever you stop a tractor-trailer. Let the truck driver choose the place to stop because of the weight load inside the trailer. It might not be safe to pull over on the shoulder of the road. He may drive another mile to the next exit. So don't get too upset and try the PIT maneuver on him. He's actually doing you a favor.

Whenever you make a stop you need to focus on what's going on inside the car. You might want to elevate your officer safety levels if you see a lot of movement. The only person that needs to get his license out of his wallet is the driver. *So why are there three backseat passengers fidgeting around?*

If you try stopping someone in a residential neighborhood and the driver doesn't immediately pull over whenever you light him up then he might live in the area. He may be trying to make it home first. I've learned from experience that some people (drunks, wanted on warrants, suspended drivers, etc.) think that officers won't tow their vehicles if they can make it home and park in their driveways.

This happened to me once in Florence, South Carolina. I noticed a guy walking out of a gas station carrying a brown paper bag. I saw him "pop the top" off of a beer bottle while I was getting gas. I observed him get into a blue van and turn into a neighborhood behind the service station. I jumped in my squad car and caught up to him. I tried to stop him but he continued driving for several more blocks until he pulled into his driveway.

He told me that he knew that he didn't have a valid driver's license. He said that he drove home because he didn't want his vehicle towed. I took him to jail and towed his vehicle anyway. Again, this is the gift that keeps on giving all day long.

I've also had people pull into someone else's driveway and pretend that they're home. More often than not, this has backfired on them whenever the homeowners came outside to see why there's a strange vehicle in their driveway with a cop car with rotating lights behind it.

The first thing that I'd tell a violator was my reason for the stop. I liked doing this on video for court purposes and to lock down my probable cause. Again, the first thing that's challenged in court by a defense attorney is the reason for the traffic stop.

I'd request one item at a time beginning with the driver's license... then the registration... then the insurance card. The reason that I liked doing this was to see if the driver was listening to me. I've had several people give me a Visa card instead of a driver's license.

I'd also wait about three seconds before taking a license from the driver. My reasoning was that I wanted to look him in the eyes... then at his hand... back in the eyes again... and back at his hand.

If his hands were shaking, I'd ask if he was on any type of medication or being treated by a doctor, physician, or pharmacist. If the driver answered "no" then he couldn't make the claim later in court that he was under the influence of medication or under the care of a doctor.

I also liked waiting three seconds to see if the motorist was so nervous that he'd throw the license at me just to get it out of his hands. It was almost as if the license was so heavy that the driver just had to get rid of it.

I liked to visually scan the vehicle as the driver searched for his information. I wanted to see if there was anything that looked suspicious inside the car. I was also looking for any weapons that could be used against me.

Take your time and *look*. I did not say "search." I can't even begin to tell you how many times that I've walked up to a vehicle and saw something illegal. It didn't matter whether it was marijuana or a weapon on the floorboard. I once stopped a driver who tried to conceal a six shot revolver with two newspapers. Unfortunately for him, the driver was also a convicted felon and I charged him under Project Cease Fire.

Other things that I'd note and liked to observe were license plates covers. Once again, a car (or any vehicle) on the roadway is like a puzzle. It'll tell a good story once you've put all of the pieces together. I also liked looking at the overall condition of the vehicle.

A traffic stop is not a drug stop. Let the traffic stop run its course and conduct your business as normal unless you see contraband in "plain view."

Conduct your business and call for a backup officer if you start seeing any items of interest.

Never talk about contraband or even ask to search a vehicle until you have another officer present. This way if you start seeing things on the traffic stop, you'll have enough time to make that call.

The three most likely times that an officer is at risk of being feloniously assaulted is at the beginning of the traffic stop; when asking for consent to search; or attempting to handcuff a subject. Every traffic cop should be aware of these three levels of threat.

When you start to question a motorist about his travel plans, make sure that the luggage matches the trip. For example, there's a case where a cop stopped a motorist on his way to Florida. He told the interdiction officer that he was meeting his family in Orlando for a vacation. His wife and three children were flying in from New Jersey. The driver had left for Florida two days after the flight and was in route with the family's minivan to meet them. However, the driver only had a backpack and a shopping bag inside the vehicle.

What made this story suspicious was that the man's spouse had to pack light so she could watch her three small children on the flight and the husband was allegedly traveling to Florida with the family's luggage. Now, you'd expect to see enough packed clothes to stay for a week in Florida.

Needless to say, the story of the family vacation was bogus and this led to a large currency seizure.

Now that we're on the topic of minivans, I want to tell you something that could possibly save your life. If you make a driver's side approach on a minivan and see that there are several people inside, *open up the gas tank door*.

The passenger in the second row will be unable to open that door. This is a factory installed safety feature that keeps the door from opening while pumping gas. Opening the fuel door may give you a few extra seconds to retreat if something goes bad. The driver would be the only person on that side who'd be able to open the door.

I hope that all of these suggestions will help you with your career. I strongly recommend the passenger's side approach. You owe it to yourself, your family, and your department to go home safe every day. As much as I love this job, I would've done it for free, but nothing is more important than family.

CHAPTER 7

THE COMPLETE ROADSIDE INTERVIEW

Before I started working interdiction, I always thought that I had pretty good interviewing skills. I went to classes whenever there was one and I watched veteran officers to see how they talked to people. I've made my share of mistakes over the years, but I had to learn on my own to be a good interviewer with very little help.

I got to be really good at reading people on traffic stops. One of the reasons that I became skilled at interviewing is that I'd ask a question and then remain quiet. I'd go about conducting my business in silence and inevitably the driver would start talking. Here's an oxymoron. In order to be a good interviewer, you have to know when to stop talking.

Think about this. It should hit home with you. Do you remember ever going to a car dealership and talking to a salesman? Can you recall sitting in his office while a dealership rep was out test-driving your car to see what your trade-in was worth. I'm convinced that they're actually holding your keys hostage because they conveniently don't give them back to you. Afterwards, the salesman comes into his office and he'll tell you what the dealership is going to offer you for your trade-in. The offer is written down on paper. He gently slides it over to you. Did you ever watch what the salesman did once you had the offer in your hand?

He didn't say a word. You see, the person who speaks first often loses. Trust me, I should know. I bought a car not too long ago and I spoke first.

This subtle technique of persuasion is still being used today by Japanese businessmen. It can be traced back to the samurai warrior's code of *bushido*. In the feudal days of Japan, when two samurais faced each other with their swords drawn, the more experienced one patiently waited for the other one to make the first move. When the inexperienced swordsman pulled back his *katana* to strike *first*, the veteran samurai would immediately counterstrike with a deathblow.

Japanese businessmen *still* follow this principle when meeting with Westerners. They'll quietly sit across the table from their Western counterparts waiting for them to speak first. This awkward silence creates an uncomfortable atmosphere. More often than not, the uneasy European or American businessmen will try to break the tension by nervously striking up a conversation. Unknowingly, they're giving the sly, oriental gentlemen the upper hand in the negotiations.

The Newlywed Effect Interview

My interview technique is very simple and easy to follow. I call it the "newlywed effect." You may remember the game show. If not, let me tell you what it was like and how it relates to my interview. Think back to when you first met the "love of your life." When you met this person there probably wasn't a day that didn't go by that you didn't see or talk to your sweetie on the phone. The first month felt like the two of you had spent a year together.

Well, the game show features four couples who are asked a series of questions. Four to the guy and four to the lady with one bonus question. Now, do you think that this was a high scoring game or a low scoring game? Please remember that these people have spent a lot of time together and have seen each other almost every day. Let me tell you, I grew up watching this game show and it was *not* a high scoring game.

You're probably wondering why I'm talking about some dumb game show. Surprisingly, I developed my interview based on the principles of this game show. My reasoning is this, *"If the people in this car just went on a vacation together then they should be able to answer basic questions about the trip, right?"*

Here's my secret. People are going to get some things wrong. Let me explain myself. If I asked you 20 questions and then asked your spouse or family member the same 20 questions, would you really get all of the questions right?

Let me remind you that I did this for a living and the answer is "No way!" Maybe you could answer about half correctly if you were really good. Okay, why then do we as cops ask someone on the side of the road eight to ten questions? And if they miss a few, we're immediately ready to tear their car apart looking for contraband... right?

Wrong!

During my interview, I'd let a few things slide. What I didn't let slide were things that people traveling together had better know. For example, "Who started driving this morning?" Only one person can drive at a time.

"Where did you stay last night?" I only asked questions where all parties should've known the answer.

Don't get preoccupied with dates, days, or times. Let me carefully explain why. If you ask two people what time they left this morning, the driver might say "Seven in the morning" and the passenger might answer "At nine a.m."

Here's what could've happened. The driver woke up at seven, showered, got dressed, loaded the car, and afterwards ate breakfast. So they didn't actually get on the road until 9:00 a.m. This happens all the time, therefore don't get caught up thinking that you have something. Limit yourself to asking questions about "morning, noon or night." This eliminates any discrepancies that a person may have with times.

People also mess up on days. For example, because I'm my own boss, today is my Friday, but to a person who works in a factory (Monday through Friday) today is actually Wednesday. I've seen this way too many times when talking to people. It's just the way that they think. The whole "art of interdiction" is the *approach* and *mindset* to catch these people lying. You can easily catch them as long as you know what kind of questions to ask.

To break this down and make it simple, always put yourself in your questions as an example.

"What did you do on your last family vacation or reunion?"

"How did you plan for this trip?"

"What time of day did you leave?"

"Did you pack food to take with you or did you stop to sit down and eat?"

"Did you trash your own car with tons of fast food wrappers?"

Here's one more way to make this easier for you. I always started off my interviews by asking questions about what had occurred within the past twenty-four hours. Where they stayed and where they last stopped.

Now I'm going to cover "clarifying questions." The last thing that you want to do is stop a car and ask a series of questions that are not related to the stop. We'll discuss more about the scope of a stop later in this chapter.

To me, the interview is everything. If you don't ask the right questions then how are you going to be able to find out if there are any deviations? If you're not interviewing then you're losing a ton of indicators of criminal activity. I don't know why, but a lot of cops are afraid to ask questions.

In court, you'll be testifying about your interview. It wouldn't be professional if you didn't talk to the violator. We've all seen "robot cops" who just walk up to a car and say, "License and registration!" I'm here to tell you that those days are long gone … or at least should be.

Passenger vehicles should be geared towards one of two things, "business or pleasure." Either a person's on a business trip or he's just joy riding.

Here are the things that you must remember while interviewing a driver on a traffic stop. You need to continue conducting business while interviewing him. For example, say that you've stopped a vehicle and asked the violator to step out of the car. As you're standing on the passenger's side of your patrol car, you inform him about the violation that you just observed him commit. You need to decide if you're going to issue a citation or cut him a warning. This is the point where I'd begin my interview.

Now, you put the violator at ease whenever you write a warning ticket instead of a moving or equipment violation. If you just told the violator that he's getting a warning and he's bouncing around, keeps touching his face, swallowing rapidly, and showing signs of nervousness then you need to key up on those behaviors quickly.

On the other hand, it's suspicious if you write a violator a six-point traffic ticket and he thanks you after you hand it to him. Why would someone thank you after being cited numerous times? Is this how a normal person reacts? No one that I know is going to be very happy about receiving a six-point ticket.

The first important thing to do is "stick to the scope" of the traffic stop. Talk about the traffic offense and tell him what he needs to do in order to correct the violation. So many times, I've seen officers stop vehicles and never talk about the violation. This is one of the worst things that you can do on a traffic stop. Always plan on everything going to court! Plan on everything that you do and everything that you say going to court.

So, what questions are you going to ask? Again, I think that the interview is everything. If you're not asking questions then you're missing the indicators.

After you've stopped the violator and advised him of the reason that you've stopped him, you need to inform him what he needs to do to correct the violation. This is where you drop your questions.

Come up with about ten good questions. As you get more experience, you can add better questions and replace the older ones. You don't have all day to talk to the violator. Some cops believe that they can ask as many questions as they want. But wait until they get into court, they'll get picked apart by the defense attorney.

When I worked interdiction on Interstate 95, I learned that most travelers were coming from New York and going to Florida. It was either spring break or a trip to Disney World. Almost everyone was on some kind of vacation.

I got to be really good at asking questions about vacations. I also got to see what behaviors were normal when people were actually vacationing. I started taking mental notes. This made it easier if I ever stopped a doper driving down the interstate with no travel plans or a "messed up" story.

Here are some questions:

"Where are you coming from?"

What gives us the right to ask this question? Well, if you stop someone for driving over the fog line, we're allowed to ask this question to see how long this person's been driving.

"Where are you heading?"

What gives us the right to ask this question? The reason is that if you've stopped a motorist from driving off the roadway then you want to see if he's physically able to continue driving.

"How long do you plan on being there?"

This question might play a better role in your interview if you discover that the driver has to be back at work by a certain day.

"Where are you staying while you're down there?"

Most trips are planned well in advance. This would let you know if the trip was pre-planned.

"Who's traveling with you today?"

I like asking this question because if a driver and passenger have been traveling together for the past ten hours then they had better know the other party's first and last name and something about that person.

"Where did you spend last night?"

Everyone in the car had better know this answer.

"Where was the last place that you stopped to take a break or get fuel?"

They had better know where they last ate and where they got gas. If this is a business trip, they should also have receipts. This is a good time to ask them if they went through any toll plazas. If they answer "yes," (which they will without thinking) ask them "Where?" This might show that they are off route or that their travel plans are not consistent with their story.

I liked asking people traveling great distances where they think that they might stop for the night if they can't make it to their destination. They should have the trip all planned out, especially if they're limited on the amount of vacation time that they get each year. For example, if the person that you've stopped only gets seven vacation days each year, then he'll have to make the most out of it. More than likely, he'll be on a schedule.

These were just a few questions that I liked asking. Now that I had a vehicle pulled over, I might generate more questions based off of what I might have seen inside the car.

If you ask everyone the same questions on every traffic stop then you're going to quickly learn what most people are going to say. Therefore, if you stop that *one car* and the driver's and passenger's answers are way off then you know that you need to spend a little more time on this particular stop.

Think about the things that you've done in your life such as moving or taking a vacation. You plan ahead and do your homework well in advance.

Here are a few things that you can use to determine if the motorist on your roadside traffic stop is hauling illegal contraband. I used to ask the driver, "Is there anything that you want to tell me about this trip?"

I've heard of cases all around the country that whenever this tactic was used, the driver would just come out and admit that he was smuggling. Either the driver just wanted to get caught and change his lifestyle or he believed that someone had "snitched" on him and he decided to come clean.

Here's another technique that I used whenever I started seeing indicators on a traffic stop. If I got to the point where I was about to ask for "consent to search," I'd say to the driver, "Is there any reason that someone would call and tell me that you're hauling contraband?"

I didn't say that anyone had *actually* called. I only made a statement. This was not a question. There is a difference! This one will trip up some of the best.

I've used this tactic from time to time and it works. There were times when I'd been on a traffic stop and found several indicators of criminal activity. I'd get written consent to search a truck and trailer. After searching the entire truck and finding nothing, I'd walk straight up to the driver and ask him point blank: "Is there anything illegal inside this truck that you want to tell me about?"

The driver would look at me, then down or away, and say, "Well, I guess you saw the marijuana inside the refrigerator…and I guess that you saw the marijuana in the ash tray… and the bottle of whiskey under the bunk."

As he was confessing like a Catholic schoolboy caught by a nun with a pack of cigarettes, I was thinking to myself, *"How in the world could I have missed all those places?"*

Well, I was a new officer back then and I often searched a little too quickly. Later, even if the driver told me where the contraband was located, I started to slow down on my searches. I still used this tactic from time to time even if I thought that I'd carried out a good search. However, I still had drivers telling me where they hid the contraband if I'd missed it. Eventually, I learned to interview better and no longer had to use this tactic.

Body Language

Whenever you're interviewing anyone suspicious, you should always be looking for *physical indicators*. You can usually tell by a person's body language whether or not he or she is being deceptive. Learn to look for the *signs!*

I eventually learned to be able to quickly tell if a driver was being deceptive or feeding me misleading answers. If you're lying, your body will betray you.

Check for a *pulsating* carotid artery. Look at the side of the driver's neck while you're talking to him. Is his carotid artery beating as if he'd just run a 400 meter sprint? I've once seen a nervous driver's carotid artery pulsating so rapidly that I could've taken his pulse without even touching him.

Another physical sign is *spontaneous sweating*. Say that you make a traffic stop and you get the driver out of his vehicle and he's sweating profusely. It's winter time. It's 30 degrees outside and cold enough to see your breath, but yet the driver's forehead is dripping with sweat.

Whenever I stopped someone who was sweating as if he just stepped out of a Swedish sauna, I'd ask him if he was under the care of a doctor. This question will protect you if the defendant ever testifies in court that he was sweating profusely because of an illness or a reaction to medication.

It's a given that most people will be nervous when stopped by law enforcement. They may start shaking, but you've got to be careful when you stop someone who's overly nervous. Just because a person is shivering doesn't mean that he's involved in criminal activity. It's when the person is so uneasy that it becomes obvious that he's up to something rotten. It's a gut feeling that you get while interviewing a driver that you start thinking, *"This is not how a normal person acts."*

If you go out today and stop twenty people, you'll begin to understand how civilians behave around cops. If you do this every day, all year long, you'll know the difference between "anxiety" and "guilty behavior." Nonetheless, you'll have to be able to *articulate* the different types of nervousness in your paperwork and court testimonies. For example, you might say something like this in court:

"Your Honor, I've made several thousand traffic stops in my career. I've run across nervous people before, but this guy was so 'nervous' that he handed me his Visa card instead of his driver's license. When I asked him for his license, he threw it at me. This person was so anxious that when he

stepped out of his car, he shit his pants and passed out."

Oh yeah! I want to welcome you to the best job in the world. This is a job where people who haul drugs will pass out on you. They'll urinate all over themselves and will often spew out projectile vomit. I've seen all of this happen during the course of a traffic stop.

If this ever happens then be sure that you *don't* tell the transport officer until *after* he's placed the soiled prisoner inside *his* patrol car and is heading off to jail. You have to have fun at whatever you do in this line of work. That's what we do!

I used to like watching a person during a roadside interview to see how many times that he touched his face or ran his fingers through his hair. It seemed to me that guilty people often channel their nervous energy by touching their faces every couple of seconds. They'll tug on their ears or rub their mustache or beard, even when they don't have any facial hair.

One of my favorite body language indicators is whenever a driver started swallowing rapidly. I'd question him about the traffic stop and before he even answered, he started trying to swallow. Then he'd swallow two or three times before answering. I've also observed a driver talking the entire time and when I'd ask for consent to search, his voice suddenly cracked or he couldn't even get the words out. He sounded like a prepubescent thirteen-year-old boy trying to ask his big sister's best friend to the junior high dance.

I was once working on I-95 and my partner stopped a van with a bunch of guys in a rock-n-roll band. Each one had his own personal baggie of marijuana. My partner lined up all of the musicians, with their hands up, alongside the road. He called dispatch for a city officer to come out and assist him. I volunteered to back him up. I was getting ready to load up the "boys in the band" in a transport van when I felt compelled to make a traffic stop. I used my emergency lights to stop a motorist for speeding. He pulled over right in front of the transport van; approximately fifty feet in front of the wagon. I called the driver out of his car and he met me in front of my transport wagon. The driver was overly nice to me as I wrote him a warning ticket. He just chatted away the entire time that I was writing the citation. He was talking a mile a minute and then he asked me, "Officer, what did those guys do to get arrested?"

His voice cracked when he asked the question. It sounded as if dust was coming out of his trachea. I told the driver that they were transporting marijuana down the interstate.

"Can you believe that someone would be that stupid to bring marijuana down the interstate?" I remarked.

He tried to reply. His mouth opened, but no words came out. It was nothing but air. He kept trying to say "No," but the words just didn't come out.

I asked him, "What did you say?" Again, he couldn't get the word "no" out of his mouth.

"Are you running dope down the highway?" I asked.

He still couldn't speak. He looked like one of those "Hungry Hungry Hippos" trying to catch a marble in his mouth. His bottom jaw seemed to be unhinged as he kept trying to form words. I immediately knew that he was guilty of something. His body language had betrayed him. He looked utterly "defeated" as he lowered his head and his shoulders slumped. My partner ran a "K-9 air sniff" and alerted to his vehicle. I arrested him for hauling marijuana. It wasn't a huge marijuana bust, but it was a classic interview.

Now I'm going to list quite a few physical indictors and try to make you aware of them. You'll see these indicators, time and time again, on your traffic stops. You need to be able to recognize them.

Physical Indicators

Are his hands shaking as he hands you his driver's license?

Does he have a pulsating carotid artery?

Is he sweating profusely?

Is he shaking?

Is he frowning?

Is he licking his lips?

Is he tugging on his ears?

Is he swallowing rapidly?

Is he "yawning or stretching?" (*It's called the "felony stretch."*)

Is he leaning on something? (*Don't let anyone ever lean on anything.*)

Is he rolling his fingers around?

Is he kicking the ground for rocks and there aren't any rocks?

Is he self-grooming?

Is he watching the road, his head swiveling around like an owl?

Are his arms crossed?

Did he go through the motions of "arresting himself?" (He automatically places his hands on top of his head or behind his back in the handcuffed position.)

Did he "shart?" (*Yes, that's what I said! When it hits cotton, you'll be able to smell it.*)

The next thing that I want to address is not only for the officer who makes the stop, but it's for the backup officer as well. You have to be on the same page with whomever you're working with. I can tell you that when I used to work with my partner, Shane, we never had to say a word to one another. We used signals! Therefore, when one of us was going to make an arrest, the other was ready and prepared to pounce.

I trust you … so I'm going to share with you our "arrest signal." It was whenever one of us scratched our badge.

A badge never itches.

First of all, be sure to watch the driver and passengers very closely as you're interviewing them. If you see one or both of them start doing stretching exercises then you might want to do some stretching of your own. You're about to chase someone down the road!

Many interdiction officers have called this the "felony stretch." If you want to make them think twice about running away then start stretching right beside them. Tell them, "If you run, it's on" and "I'm taking you down." The driver and the occupants should start thinking twice before running.

Second of all, do not let the driver or occupants lean on anything. This is an officer safety issue because the bad guy can get momentum by pushing off of a fixed object to propel his body into you in an attack.

It's a good idea to see if the driver can steady his balance unassisted. Think about this from a psychological standpoint. The weight of the crime is on the guilty driver's shoulders. It's just a matter of time before he falls over. I've seen incidents where the driver has been so nervous that he's had to grab onto something to keep his equilibrium. The smuggler knows, deep down in his heart, that it's only a matter of time before you find the contraband. The anxiety and guilt are so overwhelming that his body starts shutting down. You'll definitely want to get this on video and use it in court. If the driver didn't know that there were fifty kilos hidden inside his car then why did he pass out?

Then there are the verbal indicators that will help you on a roadside interview. A truthful response is normally short and direct. If a deceptive driver is getting ready to lie to you, he'll often take a deep sigh before answering your questions. If the driver hesitates before speaking then I'd have a "follow up" question ready; one that he should be able to answer quickly.

If you ask a driver for his license and he repeats part of the question back to you such as, "My driver's license?" I'd be prepared to ask him a *direct* question. A question that he should be able answer quickly.

If the driver says, "Oh well, I left my license at home." Then ask him his birth date. As soon as he gives you an answer like "April, 6, 1980." Ask him, "How old are you?"

I'd also ask, "What year did you graduate high school?" If he answered, "I didn't!" I'd follow up with a question like, "If you would've graduated, what year would that be?"

If you believe that he's lying then ask him, "What's your zodiac sign?" This always seemed to trip liars up; especially if the suspect was trying to give me a family member's personal information.

If the suspect didn't answer my questions fast enough (this is information that they should know immediately without having to think about it), I'd key up on that.

It's suspicious behavior, if you see a suspect doing the math right in front of you. If you watch him doing "air-math," (handwriting the figures in the air) then get ready to handcuff him. He's going to jail!

Let's say that he gets it right. Then I'd follow up with "What are the last four digits of your social security number?" Don't worry about whether you can or can't verify it. This is only a test to see how he responds to the question.

Another test that I liked using was asking the driver to spell out his full name. You'd be surprised how many people, when using a friend or family member's name, can't spell the middle or last name.

Consider looking at his cell phone and calling someone from his contact list to ask whose phone you have. I wouldn't recommend doing this technique if you're working a smuggling case, especially one involving a drug trafficking organization. It might blow your investigation.

Now, if this is your "run of the mill" traffic stop and the driver doesn't have any form of identification, then what do you have to lose? Furthermore, be careful because cops in some states can't ask for phones. According to their state's law, cell phones fall under the same category as computers. If this is true, then you'll need to get a search warrant.

The Roadside Polygraph Test

I also liked asking a series of questions in a row on a roadside interview. What I'm doing is actually a "roadside polygraph test."

Do you recall taking a polygraph when you were first hired? Well, think back to how it worked? First, they'd ask you a few basic questions about your full name, address, educational history, marital background, etc.

The "roadside polygraph test" works great on traffic stops. For example, start by asking simple questions such as

"Is this your car?"

"Where are you coming from?"

"Where are you going?"

What you're doing is building a *baseline* of how the person will answer all of the questions. This is simple to do and can also work at home with your family.

Here's an example. Say that your spouse comes home late from work. You're sitting in your big, leather recliner watching television or reading the newspaper. When your other half walks in, you ask:

"How was work?"

"How was your day?"

"How was your drive home?"

Once you've established a baseline of how your significant other is responding to your questions, it's time to ask what you really want to know.

"Did you stop anywhere?"

Watch the body language! Listen to the voice inflections to see if she's being truthful. Now you'll know what you want to know (*If she went shopping!*) and your spouse will never suspect that she was *interdicted.*

Let's go back to asking the driver questions. If the driver answers the first four or five questions the same way, it's time to throw in a question to find out what you really want to know. *Don't talk about contraband yet!* This isn't a drug stop until you start seeing overwhelming indicators, or he starts telling you a suspicious story, or starts contradicting himself. Remember what I told you? Never ask about drugs until you have a backup officer present.

If the driver answers all of your questions the same way, "yes and no," and suddenly he answers the next question with "*What?*" then you have him right where you want him.

In my experience, the word "what" has been present whenever I discovered a lot of criminal activity, especially if I asked about "contraband."

"Sir, is there something illegal inside the car that's not supposed to be there?"

"What? Inside my car?"

It's over! Go ahead and call for a case number because you're about to use it.

This was my rule of thumb when I was working the interstate and conducting roadside interviews. "No" means "no" and everything else means "yes."

This is what I mean. You ask the driver if there's any contraband inside the vehicle and he gives an answer that sounds like a machine gun *"No, no, no, no, no, no, no, no!"* Then you can be rest assured that there's contraband inside the vehicle.

If you ask the driver if there's any contraband inside the vehicle and he says, "There shouldn't be any." You know that he's lying!

Another one that I've seen was when I'd ask about contraband and the driver stopped whatever he was doing and turned around and looked at his vehicle. He stared real long and hard at the trunk of his car for a couple of seconds and turned back around and said, "No!"

I've also seen drivers turn around and look right at the trunk of a car and turn back around to face me and say, "There shouldn't be." We'd search the trunk and it was there the whole time. It's almost as if they were looking at the car to see if it was exposed.

Be sure to watch people's eyes because most of the time, guilty people will look right at where they've hidden the contraband.

Behavior Indicators or Detecting Deception

Next is a list of ways that guilty people will answer a cop's questions. You can detect deception by paying close attention to some of the things that they do.

I've come up with my own list that has worked well for me in the past on traffic stops. Again, just like the physical indicators, you have to be able to recognize these. A deceptive response will normally begin with:

Hesitating.

Deep sighing.

Repeating questions

Says "what?" after several questions. (Or "Huh?" or "Who me?").

Voice changing and cracking.

Rate of speaking picking up or slowing down.

Clearing one's throat often (*Like getting a hair ball out*).

Laughing at inappropriate things or times.

Once again, remember that you need to allow people *time* to answer your questions. Remember the

Japanese businessmen's code of *Bushido. The one who speaks first often loses.*

Here are some others:

Shifting position or changing body posture.

Saying *"no"* in a surprised way.

Saying *"no"* and then looking at you for your approval (*Did he just buy this?*).

Also, remember to listen to "disclaimer" words and phrases that people use before telling lies:

"Honestly officer, I don't do drugs."

"To be completely honest with you, I often loan my car out to all my friends."

"Truthfully, I've never been in trouble before with the law."

"To tell you the truth, I've never done drugs of any kind in my life!"

"Frankly, I had no idea that there was marijuana in my car."

"Believe me, officer. I wouldn't lie to you."

"Why would I lie to you?"

"I wouldn't lie to you officer, I support what you do. Drugs are bad."

"This is the complete and honest truth."

"What reason do I have to lie to you?"

"You're going to find this hard to believe, I do smoke some weed, but that's not mine."

"Really, you found that in my car?"

"I'm not kidding, officer. I've never seen that before in my life."

"I swear to God, officer. It's not mine, but if you let me go, I'll be at church this Sunday."

"As God as my witness, those are not my drugs!"

"To the best of my recollection, I don't *think* that anything's in my car."

"If I lie to you, may God strike me dead!" (*Hurry up and get out of there. You don't want to get hit by lightning standing next to that person*).

"I swear on my mother's grave (*who's still alive*) that's not mine!" (*Oh yeah, by the way, call the mom and let her know she's dead.*)

There are many, many more, but these are some of the best that you'll see on the road. I just wanted to hit the highlights.

I knew that I was about to hit the jackpot whenever I stopped a car that had two occupants; a male and female. I used to ask the female for consent to search and if she said, "Yes," I'd look over at the male passenger and watch for his reaction. If he was giving her the "death stare," then I knew that there was probably going to be something illegal inside the vehicle. Your backup officer will have a better view than you, so he needs to be trained to look for the reactions of the passengers.

Here's something else that you might encounter when interviewing a driver with more than one occupant. If you ask the driver if there's any contraband, he might say, "I don't have anything in the vehicle." Then the driver might take a step back leaving the other occupant or occupants standing closer to you. It's as if the driver is telling you "I don't have anything, but the passenger does." I've had this happen to me once when I was on a roadside traffic stop.

I've searched more than my share of vehicles during my career. I learned to cover all of the bases by getting the driver's consent in writing. Your video camera is a good tool, but only if it's working properly.

Now I want to caution you about consent. Make sure that you get a "yes" or a "no" whenever asking for consent. Don't take a head nod to mean "yes." Make sure that you get an answer that's understandable and can be defended in court. It's critical that if you make a major seizure it won't be suppressed because you didn't properly get consent.

Whenever I'd ask for consent to search, I'd inquire about contraband. I called it *"itemizing contraband."* I'd ask the driver "itemizing" questions such as:

"Do you have anything illegal?"

"Do you have any marijuana?"

"Meth?"

"Cocaine?"

"Heroin?"

"Ecstasy?"

"Any large amounts of U.S. currency over ten thousand dollars?"

Again "no" means "no" and everything else means "yes." You can tell what the driver is hiding inside the vehicle by "itemizing" your questions. I'd ask these questions to develop a baseline for truthfulness.

I'd key up on a driver if he gave the same answer for three of the questions and then a completely different response for another one. For example, he might look away and swallow before answering, "No...no...no...what? There shouldn't be."

I once had a case involving a semi-tractor trailer driver and when I asked him these questions, he consistently answered "no" until I asked about U.S. currency. The driver looked down and away and hesitated before answering.

"There shouldn't be any money."

I shocked him when I said, "I know that you have over ten thousand dollars inside your truck, don't you?"

The driver was giving me all of the signs that he was guilty as hell. He didn't maintain eye contact, fidgeted, had dry mouth, and was rocking back and forth on his heels. Then he answered, "Yeah, I've got quite a bit of cash in my truck."

"How much?" I asked.

"Sixty thousand dollars," he said in a trembling voice.

"Is it yours?"

"No," he paused. "I picked it up in Tampa, Florida...I'm taking it to Hugo, my boss."

I obtained written consent to search his vehicle. I decided to run a K-9 on the truck to see if the dog would give a positive alert. The dog "hit" on the tractor and then on the sleeper berth area. Inside the sleeper berth, I found a black GAP bag full of U.S. currency.

I took the money to a local bank and had it counted. It was $93,850. The driver had several different, conflicting accounts of how he acquired the money, so it was seized. The DEA in Beaufort, South Carolina picked up the case.

Most people are skeptical whenever I talk about some of the cases that I've worked that led to big money seizures. I've been asked why would a person give consent to search a vehicle when he knows that there's contraband inside it. It's easy!

This is why. Smugglers are overconfident. They're counting on officers being lazy and not bothering to search. On the other hand, a smuggler may agree to a search because he's bluffing. He's thinking to himself, *"Someone who's guilty wouldn't allow a cop to search his vehicle."* He's trying to con the officer by playing with a poker face. Deep down, he's hoping that the officer won't call his bluff. He's willing to take the chance of getting caught.

The last line of defense for a guilty driver may be that he believes that he can blame other people if he ever gets caught. He can say, "Hey, I'm just the driver." Or he'll argue in court, "Do you really believe that if I knew that there was cocaine in my car that I'd give the cop consent to search?" This is just a ploy to deflect the blame onto others.

Most people know that cops don't have time to thoroughly search every car that they stop on the road. They know that cops have to answer "calls of service" as well and this limits their time to be proactive. Therefore, whenever a cop searches a vehicle, he has to do a condensed version of the places that he'd normally look. It has to be done quickly and they search only the places that they'd look if they were only looking for the big busts.

Cops might call for a K9 officer, if one is available (they're hard to come by and always have been). If a K9 cop *is* available then the driver's in a boatload of trouble. So, in my honest and humble opinion, a driver has many more reasons to give consent than to deny it.

I can tell you that out of all of the thousands of cars and trucks that I've stopped and searched, I've only been denied a couple of times. Usually, in my experience, these guys aren't carrying and they wanted to "jerk my chain" because this time, they were empty. They wanted to *amp* me up! It's as if they wanted me to do something wrong so they could sue me later and get me in trouble.

Here's my advice on consent, car stops, and searches. Never jeopardize your integrity because integrity is *all* that you have.

Integrity is like virginity. Once it's gone, you can't get it back.

In closing this chapter on the roadside interview, here are a few things to remember.

The interview is not an interrogation.

You'll get further by being nice and professional.

Don't lie or try to trick anyone during an interview.

Remember to turn on your camera and always plan on taking every case to court.

CHAPTER 8

NO SAINTS IN DRUG TRAFFICKING

I want to start off by stating that in no way do I want to offend anyone's religious or personal beliefs. In this chapter, I'm going to cover several patron saints that are revered by smugglers within the Mexican drug trafficking organizations. Even though these drug traffickers have chosen a profession that's morally and ethically wrong, they still maintain a very strong religious belief system and are very superstitious.

It doesn't matter if you're a road officer, criminal investigator, an interdiction officer, a corrections officer on inmate intake, a narcotics detective, if you're serving search warrants on homes and businesses or pulling over vehicles, you're going to be exposed to a lot of information over your career. You need to file the following information away in your mental rolodex. It can help you identify the kind of people that you might be dealing with in one of your investigations.

These drug traffickers know what they're doing is wrong, but it doesn't stop them from praying to the saints to be sheltered from the bad acts that they're committing. They're praying to be protected from death and being apprehended by the authorities. They have strong beliefs in magic, superstition, and religious rituals. They pray for safe travels and protection when crossing the borders.

These drug traffickers pray to several patron saints. Many of these saints are legitimate and can be found in mainstream Catholicism, but these smugglers have twisted Catholicism into a "folk religion."[2] They pray to these saints and perform superstitious rituals so that these holy figures will intercede in helping them do "unholy" things.

Every one of the following "Narco-Saints" that I'll be writing about have been found on roadside traffic seizures. I have firsthand knowledge that many of these patron saints are associated with the drug trade. I've also seen them on my traffic

---

[2] Folk religion is basically made up of certain ethnic or regional religious traditions that practice under the guise of an established religion, but is outside the boundaries of official doctrine and practices. Folk religion's indigenous or native beliefs are held all over the world, particularly in parts of South America, Africa, China, and Southeast Asia.

stops. These Narco-Saints are one of the topics that I cover whenever I teach my 4:20 schools. I've asked my students during the class discussion portion about what they've seen on their roadside narcotics seizures and the feedback has been consistent all across the country. My students have found icons, prayer cards, and statues of these patron saints alongside their drug busts.

Jesus Malverde

You need to do your homework if you haven't heard of Jesus Malverde, the patron saint of drug smugglers. You'll find patron saints in Catholicism for nearly everything. There's a patron saint for police officers, fire fighters, and there's even a patron saint for gun owners. Romani gypsies even have the patron saint of thieves whom they pray to for forgiveness of thievery.

Jesus Malverde is the patron saint of drug smugglers. In the Mexican drug subculture, one can find pictures of Jesus Malverde on stickers, tee-shirts, jewelry, and prayer cards.

I want to break down Malverde's name from Spanish to English. *Mal* means "bad" and *verde* means "green." Jesus Malverde was known as the "Generous Bandit." He was an everyday Robin Hood, a folk hero to the poor. The legend holds that Jesus Malverde was one of the bandits who rode the hills near Culiacan, Mexico. It's believed that on May 3, 1909, the Mexican Government hanged him and left him to rot on a tree. Since then, every year on that date, there's been a great celebration at his shrine.

Now, I've done my research on this Mexican bandit and I've discovered that historians have never found any evidence that Jesus Malverde ever lived. They're not sure if he ever really existed, but the Mexican people believe that he did live and his Christian name was "Jesus Juarez Mazo."

Folklore holds that he was born sometime in 1870 near the town of Mocorito. They've been told that Malverde embarked on a life of crime after his parents died of starvation. According to another version of this myth, Malverde was betrayed by a close personal friend who cut off his feet. This "Judas" dragged his dead body through the hills to the local police station to collect a reward of 10,000 pesos.

One can visit the Malverde Shrine in Culiacan, Mexico. It's located near the railroad tracks on the west side of the city. This site is a well-known monument to the native people. The locals sell all kinds of Jesus Malverde memorabilia outside the memorial.

Jesus Malverde is one of the most popular Narco-Saints of all time. Many drug smugglers pray to him for protection so they can safely get their loads across the Mexican border into the United States.

It's been said that smuggling started in Sinaloa, Mexico. Allegedly, faith in Malverde is strongest for the Sinaloa people. This is one of the points of origin where many of Mexico's smugglers have emerged to become professional narcotics traffickers.

Just recently a beer was made in his honor. It's called "Malverde Cerveza" and comes in a bottle with a green label. It's been purported that 10 percent of all sales goes back to his shrine in Mexico.

I've made several traffic stops on trucks and passenger vehicles and whenever I've seen Jesus Malverde, it has usually turned into a drug arrest. Most of the time that I've seen Jesus Malverde was after I asked a traffic violator for his driver's license. I've seen the picture inside the wallet when he pulled out his license. I immediately recognized Malverde's image and knew what kind of person that I was dealing with. I've usually played dumb and asked the driver "Who's on the photo?" or "Is that a picture of your father?" The smuggler claimed that Malverde was a father or an uncle nearly every time. I always got the biggest kick out of that because "knowledge is power." I'd ask myself, *"Why is he lying to me?"* To this day, it still amazes me how many cops have never even heard of Jesus Malverde.

Santa Muerte

The next Narco-Saint that I want to talk about is "Santa Muerte." There are several different names that are associated with Santa Muerte; for example, "The Angel of Death," "Saint Death," The White Girl," "La Santa Muerte," or the "Angel of Last Resort."

There's a full-time church in Mexico City that hosts a shrine to her. The church is called *"Parroquia de la Misericordia"* ("Mercy Parish"). She has millions of followers worldwide and people pray to her for miracles or whenever they feel desperate and have lost hope. The Catholic Church in Mexico condemns the worship of Santa Muerte, but Santa Muerte worship is firmly entrenched amongst Mexico's lower working classes and "outcast" society.[3]

The truth is that the Cult of Santa Muerte actually pre-dates the Roman Catholic Church in Latin America and is older than Christianity itself.[4] It flourishes amongst Catholics because it masquerades itself as authentic Christianity.

Father Romo (Santo Toribio Romo)

Father Romo, a Catholic priest and a martyr, was born on April 16, 1900 in Mexico. He was twenty-seven years old when he was shot and killed in 1928 for being a priest during the Mexican Revolution. Mexican soldiers murdered Father Romo during the war between Catholic rebels and a government that was determined to eliminate church influence in its political matters.

Father Romo is considered by many to be the patron saint of immigrants and border crossers. He was officially canonized as a saint by Pope John Paul II on May 21, 2000.

---

[3] Gray, Steven), "Santa Muerte: The New God in Town," *Time.com*, October 16, 2007 ,
http://www.time.com/time/nation/article/0,8599,1671984,00.html, retrieved 02/05/2013

[4] Barillas, Martin, "Santa Muerte is No Saint, Say Mexican Bishops," *Spero News,* October 31, 2009,
http://www.speroforum.com/site/article.asp?id=16642, retrieved 02/05/2013

There's a belief among some Mexicans that the ghost of Father Romo has appeared to certain undocumented immigrants crossing the border and assisted them in times of their distress. He's used as an icon for hope of food, water, and money, as well as for safety.

Many drug traffickers pray to Father Romo for safe passage in crossing the border. They pray that they're able to get their vehicles across the border and into the United States without getting caught.

It's not uncommon to find prayer cards with Father Romo's picture inside a drug smuggler's vehicle. Sometimes these traffickers carry Father Romo prayer cards in their wallets or wear his picture on a necklace. These prayer cards have also been found inside containers loaded with contraband that have been shipped to other countries as well.

I recently watched one of my favorite TV shows, *The Closer*. It had a scene depicting some illegal aliens that had paid a *coyote* to bring a family across the border so they could find work in the United States. The *coyote* collected their monies and then killed the migrant workers. The television writers had thoroughly done their research. When the investigators visited the murder scene they found burning candles with pictures of Father Romo.

Niño de Atocha

Santo Niño de Atocha or "Holy Child of Atocha" is a Roman Catholic image of the Child Jesus that is popular among the Hispanic cultures of Spain, Latin America, the Philippines and southwestern United States. Niño de Atocha[5] is known as the patron saint of travelers and prisoners. You can already see where this is going.

Many illegal immigrants pray to this saint for safe passage across the U.S.-Mexico Border. The journey on foot across the border can be stifling hot and many people have died while trying.

Now think about all of the persons incarcerated on drug charges. In some places, this number is higher than almost all other crimes combined together. Keep in mind that of these crimes that are *not* drug related it's likely that most

---

[5] In Michael Jackson's video "Beat It," there's a picture of Santo Niño above his bed. On the television sitcom *George Lopez*, the Santo Niño de Atocha is prominently displayed in the family's kitchen.

offenders were probably under the influence of some type of narcotic.

Prisoners who believe that they have been falsely accused will pray to Niño de Atocha and ask for his divine help to be released from jail. I'm sure that most convicted criminals believe that they've been wronged and falsely accused, but they were tried and found guilty in a court of law by a jury of their peers.

Typically, this patron saint is shown to be a little boy that's approximately twelve years of age. He wears a pilgrim-styled hat and a very ornate cloak. He is distinctly characterized by a basket of flowers (usually roses) that he carries along with a staff and drinking gourd. He wears a cape with the shell symbol of a pilgrimage to Saint James.

Saint Jude

Saint Jude is the patron saint of "lost causes." St. Jude is a legitimate Catholic Saint. Catholics pray to Saint Jude when they're in desperate situations and when all hope seems lost, especially if a person is gravely ill. Devout Catholics might call upon St. Jude when a loved one has been taken to an emergency room with a life threatening injury.

Smugglers within drug trafficking organizations will often pray to St. Jude because hauling drugs places them in difficult situations or they know that what they're doing is a "lost cause."

I've had traffic stops where I've seen St. Jude prayer cards inside "load" vehicles. In one particular case that I worked, I stopped a driver from Texas and he told me that he owned a construction business. I noticed an American flag on the dashboard and pictures of St. Jude and the Virgin Mary above the visor.

There was a single key in the ignition. Now remember that this driver had just told me that he owned a construction business, but had only one key on his key chain. There were no tools or any construction materials inside the vehicle. There was nothing that convinced me that the driver even worked in the construction business.

I asked for consent to search his vehicle and noticed that he had strategically hung up his dry cleaning on a rack that conveniently covered up the back windows. Once I opened the back door I discovered several bundles of marijuana neatly wrapped in lawn bags. There was over eighty pounds of marijuana. Each bag contained four large packages of weed. I remember asking my partner, "I wonder how much each package weighs?" The driver, who was already handcuffed and mirandized, answered, "Ten pounds each." (*It doesn't get much better than that.*)

This person had already been caught with two prior loads of marijuana. One was for 141 pounds and the second load was 365 pounds.

If you look at a St. Jude prayer card, he'll be dressed in green and white biblical-era clothing. Jude was one of the Disciples of Christ. Most illustrations depict him with a small flame atop his head signifying the "baptism by fire" which is also referred to as the "baptism of the Holy Ghost."

You'll find St. Jude prayer cards in vehicles loaded with contraband, stash houses used by drug cartels, or in the personal property of members of drug trafficking organizations. ICE agents have even confiscated large amounts of marijuana stuffed inside large plaster statues of St. Jude along the Mexican border.

San Ramon

San Ramon is the patron saint of "secrets and silence." You can probably figure out where this is heading. Members of the Mexican drug cartels pray to San Ramon to keep their matters secret. They pray that the people within their organization will keep their mouths shut about the cartel's business.

San Ramon is also the patron saint of childbirth. It's alleged that he was born in Spain in 1204 and had to be delivered by caesarian birth. Midwives often pray to him so they can deliver babies safely.

Tradition holds that San Ramon's lips were pierced by a hot iron to keep him from preaching the Word of God. One particular ritual is centered on the padlock that is part of his martyrdom. For example, locks are placed at his altar to stop gossip, rumors, false testimonies and bad talk. They are also used to keep secrets, stop cursing or lying, and to guard priests who want to protect the secrecy of confession.

The iconography of San Ramon is pictured in the habit of his order, thirteenth century clothing, usually a white direct cloak. He is surrounded by

ransomed slaves with a padlock on his lips.

San Ramon is also the patron saint of the "falsely accused." Again, you can see why the drug traffickers pray to him. Drug traffickers will frequently rub the lips of a San Ramon prayer card to keep people from gossiping. Another "folk religion" ritual is when a practitioner will take a prayer card and place an "x" of penny tape across San Ramon's mouth to stop others from talking.

Curanderos

There are many different types of *curanderos*. These people are often respected within their communities as "natural healers." Families will call upon a *curandero* when they can't afford conventional medical treatment; however, they are not medical doctors. The word *"curandero"* is a literal translation from the Spanish word that means "healer." Their powers are considered "supernatural" as it's commonly believed that many illnesses are caused by evil spirits, a curse, or a lesson from God.

What does this have to do with drug trafficking? Drug traffickers will go to *curanderos* to be ritually cleansed of all of the bad things that they've done. They'll even ask the *curanderos* to bless their "load" vehicles before going away on a long trip or crossing the U.S.-Mexico Border.

El Niño Fidencio

Niño was one of the most famous *curanderos* that has ever lived. He was born in Guatemala in 1898. As a *curandero,* he treated thousands of people in his career. He died at age of forty. People who knew him said that he was a workaholic and worked himself to death.

El Nino Fidencio is not officially recognized as a saint by the Catholic Church. Drug smugglers often pray to him whenever they're in trouble with law enforcement.

San Simon

San Simon is another saint that's not officially recognized by the Catholic Church. He was also from Guatemala and is often confused with Jesus Malverde since they physically resemble one another.

He's known as the "Man in Black." His mustachioed appearance is one of a man in a black suit, black-tie and a hat, holding a bag of gold coins in his hands. He's the patron saint of undocumented illegal aliens, gamblers, and drunkards. A lot of drug mules are undocumented illegal aliens. They pray to San Simon for safe passage. Smugglers also pray to him for wealth and good luck in whatever they do.

Brujería

"Brujería" is the Spanish word for "witchcraft." Both men and women can be involved in practicing ritual magic. Men are called *brujos* and women are *brujas*.

The drug cartels will use *brujas* because they believe that they have the dark powers to place curses on other opposing cartel members, law-enforcement, judges or any other enemies that they might have.

Juan Soldado

Juan Castillo Morales is known by many as "Juan Soldado" (Juan the Soldier). He was a convicted rapist and murderer who later became a folk saint to many in northwestern Mexico and in the southwestern United States. Castillo, a private in the Mexican army, was arrested for the rape and murder of an eight-year-old girl from California in 1938. He was court-martialed and executed by a firing squad.

There were those who had witnessed his execution and made claims that when he was shot, the rocks around the body began bleeding. Juan maintained his innocence until his death and people believed that the Mexican Army had shot a blameless man. Shortly after his death, he had a cult following.

His devotees believe that he was falsely accused and will appeal to his spirit for help in matters of health, criminal problems, family matters, crossing the U.S.-Mexico Border and other challenges of daily life.

There are two chapels dedicated to Juan Soldado. One was built where he died and the other at the place of his burial. People still visit these chapels and pray to him. His followers are those who are having problems crossing the border into the United States and the *coyotes* who are heavily involved in human trafficking.

His prayer card icon is a picture of a man wearing a Mexican Army uniform. He's not legitimately recognized as a saint by the Catholic Church, but drug traffickers consistently pray to him for safe passage across the border.

Once when I was shopping at a Sam's Club in El Paso, Texas, I noticed a man in the checkout line in front of me. He had a tattoo on his left leg of Juan Soldado wearing a Mexican Army hat. This tattoo covered most of his leg from his knee to his ankle.

Santeria

Santeria was once called a "ghetto religion" practiced only by the inhabitants of the Caribbean Islands. These islanders were poor and uneducated, but this has all changed. Santeria is now practiced by the middle class, white, black, and Asian-Americans, as well as those from the Caribbean. There are estimates that Santeria believers now number in the hundreds of millions worldwide and it's strongly growing in the United States.

The first Santeria church to be incorporated in the United States was in 1974. It was called "Lukumi Babal Aye" and was established in Hialeah, Florida.

Santeria incorporates elements of several different faiths. It has grown beyond its *Yoruba* [6] and Catholic origins to become a religion in its own right.

It originated in Cuba when African slaves from Nigeria and Benin inter-mingled their Yoruba traditions with the Roman Catholic faith of the Spanish plantation owners. The term "Santeria" was originally a derisive word that was applied by the Spanish to mock followers who seemed to be overly devoted to the saints while neglecting to worship the Christian God.

For a long time, *Santeria* was a secret underground religion, but eventually became visible in the Americas. It spread to the United States in 1959 after the Cuban Revolution.

Santeria practitioners ritually sacrifice animals, mostly chickens, in their ceremonies. The issue of animal sacrifice was taken to the United States Supreme Court in 1993 in the case of *Church of Lukumi Babalu Aye vs. City of Hialeah Florida*. The Supreme Court ruled that the animal cruelty laws that *specifically* targeted the Yoruba practice of blood sacrifices were deemed to be unconstitutional. The Yoruba animal sacrifice rituals have seen no significant legal challenges since.

---

[6] The Yoruba religion comprises the traditional religious and spiritual concepts and practices of the Yoruba people. Its homeland is in located in Southwestern Nigeria and the adjoining parts of Benin and Togo, a region known as Yorubaland.

On January 18th 1998 in Sayville New York, Vivian Miranda, a thirty-nine year old mother from Long Island, killed her seventeen year old daughter, Charity Miranda, because she believed that Charity was possessed by a demon. Mrs. Miranda's other daughter, twenty year old Serena Miranda-Martin, held her sister down as her mother suffocated the girl during a seven hour exorcism ritual.[7]

The responding police found the mother and sister chanting and praying over Charity's lifeless body. The mother, Vivian, had recently embraced *Lukumi*.[8] However, the *Lukumi* doctrine does not endorse the existence of demons and neither does its liturgy contain any exorcism rituals. Vivian was found "not guilty by reason of insanity" and is currently confined in a New York state psychiatric hospital for the criminally insane.[9]

When I worked interdiction on I-95, I encountered many *Santeros*. There is a large Cuban population in Florida that travels up and down the interstate from Florida to New York. I've seen shrines inside cars and the offerings that they've set up in the front seat. Usually, it's a cigar, fruit or candy.

---

[7] McQuiston, John T., "Woman Who Called Daughter Possessed Pleads Not Guilty to Her Murder," *The New York Times,* January 28, 1998, p. B5.

[8] Lukumi is another name for Santeria.

[9] McQuiston, 1998

I know an officer who once stopped a vehicle with Florida tags. The male driver was of Cuban descent. There was an ornamental chest inside the vehicle's trunk; decorated like a pirates' treasure chest. The officer looked inside the coffer and found a chalice of chicken blood and a freshly severed chicken's leg. A pair of plastic handcuffs was also inside the chest. I suppose that this was a protective form of magic in case the driver was stopped by law enforcement.

My advice is that you never take anything out of the offering plate ("treasure chest"). I know a Palm Beach County (Florida) deputy that once searched a car and found a cigar in an offering plate sitting on the front seat. This "cigar" was an offering to whatever deity the driver was trying to appease. The deputy thought the cigar was rubbish and flung it out on the ground. *The fight was on!* This deputy had disrespected the driver and didn't even know it.

Don't put yourself in a situation like this. If you see something that you don't understand then ask the driver about what you're looking at. More than likely, he'll tell you what it is if Santeria is the religion of his or her choice.

I challenge you to learn more about each saint that I've listed in this chapter. Never stop learning!

I also want to encourage you to share this information with the other officers in your department. I'm sure that they've seen these saints and offerings before, but had no idea of what they were looking at or understood the meaning behind them.

Bob Marley and Scarface

The next two icons that I want to talk about are not patron saints, but they're something else that I used to see in either cars or residences of drug traffickers. The first is "Bob Marley" and the second is "Scarface." Ask your local narcotics officers how many times that they've seen pictures or references to Bob Marley or Scarface when they've been carrying out search warrants.

The Three-Legged Pig

Another image that I used to see was a ceramic or clay "three legged pig."[10] The origin of

---

[10] The creation of the three legged pig originates from a village in Pomaire, Chile where it is the custom to offer a three legged pig as a gift for a friend or family and for ushering good luck and good will.

this pig is from the country of Chile. It's called a *"chanchito."*

Why does the pig only have three legs?

Well, the theory behind this is that a three-legged pig is a good luck charm when traveling (so that they won't get stopped by law enforcement). The reason that the pig's leg is missing is that some Chilean family loved this little pig so much that instead of killing him, they cooked and ate only one leg. Therefore it's a "lucky pig."

I once stopped a kid in Myrtle Beach, South Carolina and when I approached the car on the passenger's side I noticed that there was a wooden pig in the cup holder. I asked the driver for his license, registration, and insurance card. Then I asked, "What's that in the cup holder?" He looked at me and answered:

"That's a pig…pig!"

"Oh! It's on now," I thought to myself.

Well, this was supposed to be his good luck charm, but it didn't work out too well for him in the end. It still had a price tag on it and I charged him with "possession of marijuana."

CHAPTER 9

Searching Techniques

I want to start off by saying that if you don't know how to take vehicles apart then you need to enroll in a training class that teaches cops how to properly search vehicles. The last thing that you want to do is tear apart someone's vehicle or get hurt in the process. If you don't know what you're doing, then ask someone.

Take my advice and grab some tools, go to a junkyard and make your mistakes there. Even more importantly, if you tear up someone's car then your program could get shut down. Get out there and learn how to do it the right way.

Since I became an interdiction officer, (and now an instructor) I've done my homework. I've discovered that most hidden compartments are on the driver's side as compared to the passenger's side. If you think about it, one of the reasons that we don't spend as much time searching the driver's side is because of the danger of passing traffic. "Officer Safety" has been burned into our minds. We know that we're safer if we spend more time searching the passenger's side.

Think about the last time that you searched a car. Was the driver watching your every move? They watch and learn from us. They're watching how we conduct our searches. They know that we're always looking over our shoulders for oncoming traffic.

You'll search a lot of vehicles over your career. The more vehicles that you search that *need* to be searched, the better you'll get at searching vehicles. Did you notice that I said "the vehicles that *need* to be searched?"

If you're searching every automobile that you stop then you need to quit doing this! I hope that after you've read the chapter on "possible criminal indicators" you'll know which vehicles that you need to spend more time searching.

What I liked doing whenever I searched a vehicle was to always start in the same place unless the driver indicated an area that I needed to focus my attention. For example, say that I asked the driver, "Is there anything in the vehicle that's not supposed to be there?" and he turned around and looked back at the trunk. Now that was the area where I needed to start.

Take the time and ask drivers these questions and pay close attention to their body language. They'll tell on themselves!

Learn a search pattern and stick to it. I made sure that I was in a safe location before I ever searched a vehicle. I never wanted to search an automobile that was on the fog line of a major highway or interstate. If I believed that the traffic stop was going to be more than a simple warning or traffic citation, I'd ask the driver to move the vehicle off the roadway so we didn't get hit. Another reason that I'd do this was to signal my partner who was in the middle of the highway watching traffic. When he'd see me move the vehicle off of the shoulder then he knew that he needed to come and assist me. He'd respond without me ever having to call him on the radio.

I liked to start off on the driver's side and work my way around the entire vehicle. The reason that I preferred to start on the driver's side is that the driver is usually within arm's reach of his contraband. This would be the personal user amounts of narcotics such as joints, dime bags, small amounts of cocaine, crack or methamphetamines, or a meth or crack pipe with residue.

Another reason that I'd like to start searching the driver's seat area was because once I found something illegal, I was now in control of how long it was going to take me to complete the search. This is especially true when you're working off of "consent to search." Remember, the driver can withdraw his or her consent at any time.

I'd scan the entire area as I sat in the driver's seat. I'd take a second to process everything that I was seeing. I'd look for signs of wear and tear. Remember that the interior of most new cars are made out of plastic. People who take off these plastic parts don't always line everything back up before putting the panels back. They'll often "fist-hammer" them back into place. When this happens, small pieces often fall off onto the carpet and onto the next lower panel.

I also liked to look at the speedometer housing unit. One of my favorites is the Jeep Laredo. On most models, the speedometer housing lifts straight up and out and the bad guys can hide their pistols inside the cavity. They now have access to their guns in less than a second. I have five "concealment videos" on my website and the Jeep Laredo is featured as one of the twenty vehicles on the "Passenger Vehicle" DVD.

I also liked looking at all of the vents while shining my flashlight inside or I'd remove the whole vent all together. Most of these vents will just pop off and are easily assessable to search.

The inside trim pieces, right up against the window, are also made of plastic. They likewise pop on and off and I've found quite a bit of user amounts of dope inside there.

One of the oldest tricks in the book is the seatbelt assembly. A doper will take a small amount of drugs and tape it to the seat belt so in case they get stopped by law enforcement they can remove the seat belt and it'll slide back into the seat belt housing unit. *Pretty clever, huh?*

Don't forget about the radio. You'll need a pair of radio pullers to get access behind the dashboard. It's a lot easier to remove the radio in two seconds then trying to remove a bunch of screws.

Now I want to let you in on a secret about smugglers and drug users. They're normally lazy and they'll hide their drug stash quickly and easily. Why take off ten screws when they can remove a plastic panel (like on the Jeep Laredo) where it can be quickly accessed? Think like they do and you'll make more dope cases.

Look for hidden stashes inside cup holders or the center console area. Search on-line for "stash hides." One website that I've found to be helpful is at www.bewild.com. Here's my advice, use a government computer when searching it. You'll see several hundred types of hides that dopers are currently using to fool officers. You'll see what they're spending their money on to hide their drugs from cops. Be ahead of the ball game and keep doing your homework. Pass this information on to all of your coworkers. Chances are that they've seen these before, but didn't know what they were seeing.

For example, there are coffee mugs sold with false bottoms. The coffee cups can hold hot steaming coffee in the opened top portion while the drugs are hidden in the lower area. On a car stop, a doper can show you his bogus coffee mug and ask for permission to drink his coffee as you're searching his car. As you're finding indicators of drug use while searching the vehicle, the doper is standing outside, sipping his coffee, and smirking at you. What you didn't know was that the drugs were in the false bottom compartment the entire time.

A jar of peanut butter is another place where I liked finding dope. Drug users will take a brand new jar of peanut butter and remove some of it with a spoon. They hide the dope inside and spoon the peanut butter back on top. Then they microwave the jar for about five seconds. The peanut butter will smooth out again as if no one had ever tampered with it. Next they'll super glue the lid in three or four places and the peanut butter jar looks brand new.

The area around the gear shifter will pop out in most passenger vehicles. You can look down towards the bottom region of the dashboard and also back towards the backseat area. The molded cup holder usually comes out as well.

Closely examine the carpeted area near the gas and brake pedals. If you see small loose grey insulation pieces on top of the flooring then you know that someone has pulled the carpet back. You need to look at this area very meticulously. Look at the bolts holding the seats in for any tool markings while you're down there. If you find tool marks then it's a clue that the seat has been taken out and you might have a secret floor compartment.

It should also be noted that the carpet should *not* be glued down. Look underneath the vehicle for any rust marks or rough edges. When automobiles leave the factory's assembly line they don't have rough edges. Everything should be at 90 degree corners.

Don't take it personally if another officer shows up on your traffic stop to help search and finds something that you missed. Two officers are allowed to search, but *only* if there's another backup officer to watch the driver. Backup officers are *never* allowed to search. That's not their job so don't allow them to do this. I know that they want to assist you, but this is not helping either one of you.

Your backup officer should be watching the violator's body language as you're searching the vehicle. More than likely the violator will be watching you while you're searching the car. Say that when you reach the trunk area, the violator now lays his face in his hands and looks up as if he's praying. Your backup officer needs to let you know what's happening. He should alert you that you need to pay real close attention to the trunk area.

If you're not using a flashlight when searching vehicles then you're missing it! It doesn't matter if it's sunny outside and you have plenty of natural sunlight. You still need to use a flashlight. You should be looking for dust disturbance or fingerprints when examining the dash vents. I also liked using my flashlight to look at the screw heads to see if anyone had tampered with them.

Another physical criminal indicator is a black or silver Sharpie marker inside a vehicle. Smugglers will paint the screw heads back to the right color with a Sharpie after they've tampered with them. I also like taking my finger and touching the screw heads to see if they're rough. It doesn't matter if the screw heads have been painted or not. They can't cover up the fact that the screws had been tooled and have rough edges.

Try to use all five of your senses when searching. Use your eyes more than your hands. Don't put your hands inside anything that you can't see. Pick up a small search mirror and use it to look inside those spaces.

Backseat Area

Let's move into the backseat area and start searching. The first thing that I liked doing was to remove the backseat. Not all backseats come out. They're bolted down, but most seats pop out easily. This will give you a better view and will open up the search area. Check inside the foam area of this seat before moving on to the next.

Once the seat has been removed, I liked examining the sending unit. The "sending unit" is the top of the fuel tank. Chances are that no one's tampered with it if there's dirt and grime on top. I was suspicious if I ever discovered that it had been cleaned and wiped down. You don't have to worry about fuel being spilled when you open this area.

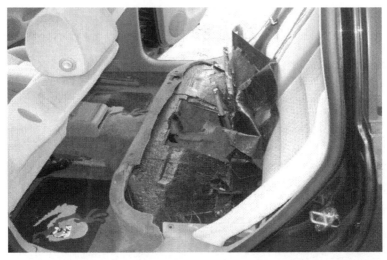

Warning: Be sure to always check the owner's manual first. Car manufacturers change the designs of their vehicles all the time. I've done this countless times and have never experienced any problems. Smugglers can gain access to this area and float their drug packages.

The seat backs are another place that has nice sized voids. Be careful if you've never removed one of these seat backs. Get your experience in your impound lot or at a local junkyard. The last thing that you ever want to do is destroy a citizen's vehicle or a seized vehicle. The whole idea of taking care of these vehicles (if they've been involved in criminal activity) is that your department can sell these cars later and get the most money possible out of them.

A good place to pull the carpet back and look for hidden compartments is at the backseat lower base area where the carpet stops. The Volkswagen Jetta or Passat are well known for compartments in this area. Remember that it's a clue if the carpet has been glued down. Most of the ones that I've seen are on the driver's side. I've only seen a couple in the center region which are easier to find if the seat has been removed.

The best place to look for any wires that are used with a hidden compartment is on the driver's side near the backseat and trunk area. You'll get your best results by removing the weather stripping or the plastic panel (called the "kick plate") at the door.

While you're in the backseat area, check the base of the rear center console. The Chrysler 300, for example, has a nice sized natural void.

Some cars have a center console armrest with cup holders that fold up. The area behind this armrest leads into the trunk. Carefully examine these cup holders. Most of them pop out. Behind the armrest, in the part that meets the trunk wall, there are some plastic clips. They can be removed and you'll find a nice voided area inside the armrest.

Look up at the ceiling and check for any vents. Most of these vents can be removed. For example, minivans have several ceiling vents. This would be a good time to get out your small mirror and look around.

While in the backseat, check the front seat headrests. Then turn around and check the backseat headrests.

Check both doors before getting out of the backseat. Shake them to feel if they weigh heavy. You should also roll down all of the windows to make sure that everything works properly.

Trunk Area

Once you're finished with the driver's area and the backseat, it's time to move to the trunk. After I popped the trunk, the first thing that I liked looking at was the rear bumper. I'd look for tool markings on the bolts or plastic pushpins. It's probably been removed if this area has been "tooled." You can't see this unless you've opened up the trunk. I'd remove the plastic panel that covers the trunk latch if I ever found tool markings. I'd use an upholstery tool to remove all of the plastic clips. This is the best way to look at all of the voids.

If you have a car that has pointed tail lights, then make sure that you search the rear corners. Some have deep voids. You have to go into the trunk, reach in and rotate your arm and hand and bring it back towards you. These are good sized voids. This area is also how one can access the rear tail lights on some cars.

Check the spare tire and make sure that it matches the car. Note: a minivan's spare tire can be located up front beneath the middle of the driver's seat and passenger's seat. You'll have to go through the center console area to remove the spare tire. Read the owner's manual for more information.

A minivan's spare tire has a plastic shell cover that is huge and can carry quite a bit of contraband once the tire has been removed. This shell is secured under the van's floor and is easily accessed. Most cops think that there's a false floor if a K9 shows interest underneath the minivan. Always check the spare tire!

If there's a battery in the trunk area, then examine it as well. For a long, long time, smugglers have been using fake batteries to hide contraband.

Warning: be careful when touching a battery. If you don't know what you're doing, then ask someone. Don't ever put yourself in harm's way.

Don't forget about the rear speaker deck. For example, the rear deck is held up by plastic clips on the Chrysler 300. Remove these and you'll find a large void area.

Engine

I'm aware that most officers don't search engines or beneath vehicles. It may be because officers don't want to get dirty or maybe they can't squeeze themselves underneath. Most cops are big people. Trust me, I know. I sell law enforcement t-shirts and most of the sizes are XL and up.

You can see most hidden compartments from beneath the vehicle. That's why in the section on "pre-patrol preparations," I talked about finding a business that will allow you to use its lift if you ever need to move a vehicle in order to get a better look. But first, check with your department and see what the policy says.

Check the fluids whenever you're searching the engine as these areas are getting popular with transporting controlled substance such as pills or ecstasy. I call these sorts of smugglers, *"Pillbillies,"* because they drive down from the Midwest to Florida to "doctor shop" for pills. Then they drive back home to sell them.

Smugglers are also using bike tubes and black wire looms to camouflage their drug stashes. They look just like factory parts. If you're searching a *rental vehicle* then you should be suspicious of any signs of activity under the hood. Again, have you ever looked in the engine area of a rental vehicle when you rented a car?

After you've opened the engine hood, look to the right and left at each side of the fender wells. Each fender well usually has four or five bolts. You should be looking for signs of tool markings that the bolts have been removed.

Don't forget to check the air filter. Likewise, examine the area around the windshield wipers. They're usually pinioned on by plastic push pins and are very easy to remove. These areas have deep natural voids.

I once taught a class in Texas and on the very first day a trooper went to lunch, stopped a car on his way back, and made a seizure after he searched the window wiper area. This student made a currency seizure during the first class of our school. Great job, trooper!

What I've seen lately is that smugglers are now storing liquid methamphetamine and PCP in the windshield wiper fluid container. On our website www.the420group.com, we post all of our intelligence bulletins. Stay informed and updated. You can also post some of your own on there to share with other cops. Our website is free and we don't and will never charge for using it.

Now I want to point out a few key areas that should be searched underneath the vehicle. Don't be afraid to go under the car and get down and dirty. The hog head, also known as the "differential," should be looked at for fingerprints and any disturbance. Smugglers will hollow these out and transport contraband inside this area. Be sure to also check the spare tire and the front and back bumpers.

A few years ago, the newly assembled Ford Taurus had a factory void that came right off the assembly line. For a while, smugglers took advantage of this until word got out to law enforcement. They built a trap beneath the vehicle and put a trunk's latch to secure it. It's located between the back rear axles. It's almost dead center in the middle.

Keep in mind that rust marks are indicators when you're looking under a vehicle. Another indicator is if it's dirty everywhere but one spot. Also, be sure to check for factory edges.

Rear Cargo Area

Here's what you need to look for if you want to find a hidden compartment in the cargo area of an SUV. If you measure six inches to a foot behind the back seatbelt assembly, towards the back cargo area, you'll find an entrance to a hidden compartment.

For example, Ford Explorers, Ford Expeditions, and Toyota Four-Runners are famous for their rear cargo compartments. These sections open up from the front of the vehicle and lift back towards the rear. I've only seen a few that are opened the opposite way.

Mitsubishi Montero Sports SUVs are famous for having great roof compartments. They're located inside the vehicle. They can be found by removing the plastic push pins that hold up the headliner. Another great concealment area is in the second row of seats. Flip up the seats forward and you'll find an access point to a trapdoor near the seatbelt assembly that's attached to the frame. It's within six inches towards the rear cargo area. An indicator of potential drug smuggling would be if the carpet has been glued down beneath the seat. This is the same for Ford Explorers, Expeditions, Four-Runners and most cargo sport utility vehicles.

Ford Excursions, Lincoln Navigators, Cadillac Escalades, and Nissan Armadas are well-known for front and backseat center consoles that can be used for hidden compartments.

You need to learn about all of these vehicles if you want to be good at finding contraband. Don't worry about how to open up these compartments. Studying to understand which wire does what can be time consuming, but it's pretty neat to see how they work.

Let's talk about the rear defrost unit. Most smugglers will use the rear defrost wire to jump off of to use for hidden rear compartments. Here's the reasoning: Why risk being discovered by law enforcement by running a wire from the front of the vehicle to the back when there's a factory issued one already in place?

The last thing that I want to talk about is the glove box and the airbag. Check to see if the driver has turned off the passenger's side airbag. This would be suspicious if there was another adult passenger riding in the car.

The glove box is easy to search, but here's what you're looking for. When you drop a glove box there's usually a string that keeps the glove box from dropping all the way to the floor. If you notice that this piece is missing then you know that someone has tampered with it. This is suspicious especially if it's inside a rental vehicle. Why would anyone need to drop a glove box in a rental vehicle?

Learn about the natural void spaces in these vehicles! They're going to be the same places where smugglers are going to hide their contraband.

I hope that this chapter has helped you with how you approach interdiction. You'll develop your own style and you'll get better with time. Try to enroll in as many schools as possible. Work with as many people as you can to see how they work. Share information and always network with other officers. Remember you're only one stop away from being in the top one percent of our profession.

Happy Hunting!

CHAPTER 10

Bulk Currency Seizures

It's not against the law to have over ten thousand dollars in your possession. You could have just sold your Harley Davidson or your Winnebago motorhome. We never arrested people in South Carolina for having $10,000 in cash, even when we could prove that it was drug money. However, we *did* start up an investigation and called in the feds to assist us with our cases. Later on down the road, they were indicted. You always let the mouse run home to see where the home is located.

You need to have a nexus in order to seize currency. For example, say that you stop a person driving a broken-down truck. The driver has three prior drug trafficking charges and you find $100,000 wrapped in duct tape inside a duffle bag lying in the front seat. You can seize the currency because you can prove that this person has a *nexus* with prior trafficking.

I've made my share of currency seizures when I worked in South Carolina. State law allowed us to seize any monies over a thousand dollars if it was in close proximately to drugs. I loved making cases where I found a small amount of marijuana and the person had two thousand dollars cash on him. If you can do this 100 times during a calendar year, that's $200,000 that'll go into the state's asset forfeiture account!

The reason that it had to be at least a thousand dollars before we could seize it was because that's what it cost to file for the assets. Subsequently, if we confiscated $1,001 with a marijuana case, we would only receive a dollar in our account. However, the amount of money never matter to me. Here's the way I viewed it. I did my job and the bad guy lost over a thousand dollars. It hurts when you're a drug dealer and your drug money is taken away.

I remember the time that I stopped a guy who just got his tax check back that day. Unfortunately, he had some marijuana in his possession. I stopped him across the street from a school. *Ouch!* "Possession with Intent to Distribute (marijuana) in a School Zone." We delivered a knockout punch when we seized his $3000 tax check.

I used to get just as excited with the small drug cases as I did with the big ones. I'm "zero tolerance" on any amount of drugs! My thought process is, "If they'll smoke a little, then they'll smoke a lot."

Let's go right into covering traffic stops with currency seizures. I'll teach you everything that I know and what we used to do when we worked the street. I strongly suggest that you talk to your local prosecutor and go over what I've covered to see if you have to do things differently in your state. The last thing that you want to do is make a good stop, seize the money, and have to return the dope money back to the dealer or smuggler. Once again, I'm going to only offer you some suggestions. It is your responsibility to make sure you're within the legal ends of your jurisdiction.

Please keep in mind that it's a *crime scene* if you stop a car, search it, and find currency.

I never handcuffed a suspect after I found currency. I almost did once and was stopped by a veteran officer who said:

Wait…wait…wait!!! Let's just go over and read him his Miranda warnings and talk to him."

I was ready to take him to jail for money laundering, but I learned a valuable lesson that day from a great cop who was used to making big money seizures. This driver was supposed to be traveling from New Jersey to Florida to buy cars for a dealership. He had $86,890 in a shoe box, a TCH test kit, and a *High Times* magazine.

Don't call *everyone* on your shift to come out to your traffic stop. Request two backup officers at the most. Don't pull out the currency and start stacking it up on the hood of your car. Again, this is a crime scene and needs to be treated as such.

First, call for a K9 officer before you take out your camera and start snapping pictures of where you found the currency. Why? Because if you call the DEA or any other federal agency about this money seizure then they're going to want a police dog to run around the car and get a positive alert on the money.

Don't touch the money! Once you've searched the car and discovered the money... stop right there! Back out and then call for the dog.

Also make sure that the video camera in your car has enough storage space because you're going to be there for a while. If there's any question then I'm going to suggest that you call for another car with a dashboard camera. Have that officer park his car behind yours just in case your camera stops taping. This way, you have backup footage while you're changing out to a new tape. Once you've changed the tape it's a good idea to have the second vehicle get a better view of your car and the crime scene. This would be more of a behind the scenes view.

After the K9 officer has arrived, be sure that you *don't* tell him that there's money in the backseat. Let the K9 team do their jobs. Besides, how would this look on video in case it goes to court?

Make sure that you get a copy of the K9 report for your files after the dog has alerted on the currency and the K9 handler is finished.

Just a note, some police departments, in similar situations, will take the dirty money out and place it in a lineup with the luggage and other contents inside the vehicle. Next they'll add the clean bag of money in the lineup so that the dog can make a run on all of the items. Then they'll video record the handler running the dog around the car a second time to show that the dog alerted on the drug money and not the clean money.

I've never done this, but I've known of other departments that make this a standard procedure. Make certain that you also use latex gloves when handling the money so that you don't contaminate the clean money.

Always wear gloves when dealing with contraband. I want to tell you about two friends of mine who are incredible interdiction officers. They once made a traffic stop that resulted in a major currency seizure. What they didn't know was that the Cartel had put a thin powdery substance on the packages. The two officers became sick. Deathly sick!

They were rushed to the emergency room. One of the officers was in the hospital for several days. This officer was surrounded by his family and it got to the point that he filled out his will. Can you imagine what he was going through as he lay upon a hospital bed, filling out his will, with his family in close proximity? Fortunately, both officers made a full recovery, but what that substance was, no one ever knew. Therefore, it's of the upmost importance that you wear your gloves when searching for contraband. Your number one priority on any traffic stop or drug interdiction stop is that you safely go home to your family each and every night.

Here's one more story. The same thing happened to another southern state police agency. There were a couple of troopers who discovered contraband during a traffic stop. The troopers transported the drugs to their central evidence facility. They were assisted by several other troopers and staff members in entering the narcotics into evidence. The packages were covered with some type of pesticide and it sent more than seventeen people to the emergency room.

Upon *mirandizing* the driver, you should inform him that the money is going to be seized pending an investigation. The next thing that you want to do is try to persuade him to write out a statement for you. Ask him to voluntarily follow you back to the office for the statement. Now, you're probably thinking that there's no way that this person would ever consider doing this. Nonetheless, from my experience, I can tell you that not only will the suspect voluntarily follow you back to your office, but will also go with you to the bank to get a receipt for the monies.

The drug mule will want to take something back to the drug trafficking organization to show that the money has been seized by law enforcement. The smuggler's life is in peril if he ever returns back to the drug trafficking organization without a receipt.

Many years ago if a drug smuggler refused to fully cooperate with a federal drug investigation then the feds wouldn't give him a receipt for any seized monies. You can probably imagine what happened when he returned home. I'm sure that there were a lot of smugglers back then who decided that it was in their best interest to cooperate with a federal investigation.

If you ever make a significant currency seizure and call for a K9 officer then you should also get the Drug Enforcement Administration involved as well. These DEA agents will want to interview any smuggler right after they've written out their statements.

If a smuggler is not willing to write out a statement, then ask if he'd be willing to talk to you inside your car with your video camera recording the conversation. There are times that a smuggler won't write out a statement, but will prefer to talk to an officer on video instead. What he's thinking is that the last thing that he wants floating around is a piece of paper with his name on it.

Many times members of these drug trafficking organizations go to court so they can learn the facts of how they were stopped and how the officers found the contraband. Actually, they had no intention of ever fighting the drug charges. The courtroom is a classroom. They want to get better at their trade by going into the mind of their enemy. In essence, they're "paying" for the information now so they can correct their mistakes in the future. This happens all the time in our line of work.

Don't bring the money back to your car and put it in evidence bags! You don't want to put bagged currency in your car and have one of the packages slide under your seat. If this happens, you just opened a can of worms. Again, don't take the currency back to your vehicle. Always have two officers present whenever you're handling money.

As soon as I knew that there was a money seizure as a result of my traffic stop, my next phone call was to my supervisor (after calling the K9 and the feds). I wanted to get him headed to my location.

After you've removed the "bagged and tagged" currency from the violator's car and placed it in the front seat of your patrol car, you need to turn your dashboard camera around and place it on the evidence bags of money. Leave it there and stay off of your phone! This isn't the time to call your buddies and tell them about your big bust.

Once you've left the traffic stop, ask the officer behind you (who's also videotaping) to follow you to the office or bank. Be sure that when you get there you have the video rolling and a supervisor on scene. I've discovered that this worked best for me whenever handling currency. My back was covered by a supervisor and dashboard video footage. Find out what your policy says about handling currency and contraband. Take the necessary steps to protect yourself and your agency from any frivolous accusations and lawsuits.

It's not our job to count currency during a roadside seizure. There are too many distractions and too many opportunities for things to go wrong. Instead, take the money to a bank and let them count it for you. This way, both you and the violator get an accurate amount of the exact currency from the bank. I've heard of cases where officers had miscounted the money, issued a receipt, but the tally was wrong. This could've been prevented by following the above steps.

If the nexus between the currency and a violator is a prior drug charge then print out the record of the criminal history and include it with your case file and police report.

Never get in a hurry on any seizure! It doesn't matter if it's drugs or U.S. currency. Practice these steps and it'll become second nature.

Everybody at your traffic stop must be on the same page.

Do not take trophy shots of the money or dope on the hood of your squad car as your dashboard camera is recording. This is not the time or place to do this… and it's definitely not professional.

If you're going to be doing this kind of work, then request that your department pick out a bank and inform them about what you're going to be doing. The bank has to be on the same page as well.

Some police agencies even have bank accounts set up so that they can safely and responsibly deposit the monies. Whenever we seized money and transported it to a bank, we'd have the bank write a check to the U.S. Marshals. You should make sure that the feds will adopt your criminal case before you ask the bank to cut a check to the Marshals. Nothing is more embarrassing than authorizing the bank to write the Marshals a check and then the case doesn't go federal. Well, good luck with this cluster and remember what I've said before, "Take your time!"

Here's another cautionary tale. Whenever we confiscated monies and went to the bank to get it counted, a bank official usually asked me (or my counterpart) for my social security number. At first, I had no problem giving them my social security number, but what I didn't know was that each time I deposited over $10,000, the bank notified the Internal Revenue Service (IRS). I later found out that I could be held accountable for the taxes on these monies. Just think about it. What if I was audited by the IRS and they looked into all of the counter deposits I had made over the last five years. This would've opened up all sorts of problems for me and my family. I would have been able to clear my name, but think about all of the hours that I would have lost trying to document that all of these deposits were legitimate.

This is why your department should set up a bank account in advance. This is why you should not give the bank your social security number whenever you're depositing drug monies. The workers at the bank are set in their ways when it comes to filling out paperwork, but depositing seized drug currencies are different. Any deposit over ten thousand dollars is automatically reported to the IRS.

Seizure Recap

Where was the money or drugs found?

How was the money or drugs packaged?

Was the currency wrapped with rubber bands?

What amounts were in each bundle, ten thousand, twenty thousand, etc.?

What were the denominations of the bills; twenties, fifties, or hundreds?

Were the bags vacuumed sealed? Was there a masking agent used on the packages such as mustard, grease, etc.?

Were dryer sheets used to mask the odor?

Vehicle Information

Who's the registered owner of the vehicle?

Was the registered owner present?

Note: Was the vehicle recently purchased? It might be in your best interest to find out who was the previous owner.

Cell phones

Does the driver have a cell phone or mobile phone? Try to do a "phone dump" if state law allows it. On the other hand, you might want to play it safe and get a search warrant. All recent calls, text messages, and photos could be very important to your case.

K9s

Was a K9 used?

Did the K9 alert to the vehicle? If so, where on the vehicle?

Exactly where did the K9 alert inside the automobile?

Did you use clean money along with the violator's money? To which one did the K9 alert?

Did you get copies of the K9 officer's report and video?

Did you get video copies of every officer on the scene that used a camera?

Did you get supplement reports from every officer on scene without a camera?

Did you print out the suspect's criminal history and driving record?

Did you get a signed copy of the written consent form?

Did you get a signed copy of the written Miranda Warning (or Spanish Miranda Warning)?

Other Items of Interest

Did you find any receipts inside the vehicle?

Did you make a copy of all of the items that you found inside the vehicle such as credit card receipts, credit cards, prepaid calling cards, and any papers with the driver's handwriting including phone numbers or notes? Any bank statements or ATM receipts that the driver might've had? "One person's trash is another person's treasure."

You need to be looking for any information or documents inside the vehicle with someone else's name on it. You're required by law to notify that person (or make your best attempt) to see if he or she may have a legal claim to the money.

For example, say that you stop a vehicle and find currency during a consensual search. The driver is not the registered owner, but you find mail belonging to Joe Smith and Sally Smith's driver's license. You now have to send them a certified letter notifying them about the recovered monies.

I once made a significant money seizure of about $35,000. There were three people inside the car and all three had different stories about what they were doing, where they were going, and how they obtained the money. All three had prior drug trafficking charges.

While searching the car, I found an elderly lady's driver's license. I soon learned that the little old lady had passed away three days earlier. I called the Boston Police Department and told a BPD detective what I had at my traffic stop. No one inside the vehicle was gainfully employed and all three were going to Florida for about a week.

Upon further investigation, I discovered that the driver was on parole for "drug trafficking." He wasn't even allowed to leave the state of Massachusetts. I gladly faxed my police report to his parole officer. The Boston Police Department soon opened a case on the deceased elderly lady. These three outstanding citizens were all suspects in her death.

I hope that these suggestions will help you whenever you make a currency or dope seizure. If you want to learn more about commercial vehicles then check out my book entitled, *It's 4:20 Somewhere: Professional Commercial Vehicle Interdiction* (2014).

Please remember that you have the best job in the world, but your family should be the most important thing to you in your life. Stay safe out there and may God bless you.

Chapter 11

My Personal Stories

This next chapter features the personal stories of James Eagleson while working in his law enforcement career as a police officer. We all have stories that'll stick with us for the rest of our lives. I want to share some of these stories that I'll never forget with you. This is the best job on earth!

Caution: These stories are now several years old and may not be exactly as accurate as I remember. As fish stories grow, I think that these stories did as well. Enjoy them…and remember that this is how I recall them.

The Stolen Car Idiot

One of the things that I often think back on during my career was a stolen vehicle case that I worked. I was a city police officer in North Charleston, South Carolina. During the Field Training Program, I was placed with a very seasoned veteran officer. He was very good at his job and I really did learn a lot.

One time, we were patrolling a neighborhood when we drove through an apartment complex and noticed a vehicle with Connecticut plates. For the past several weeks, we had always made our rounds through these apartments and had never noticed this car before. It was suspicious; a brand new car in a rundown apartment complex. I ran the tag and sure enough it came back as "stolen."

It was bright and early on a hot steaming day as I was standing outside of my squad car in the hot South Carolina sun. Sweat was running down my spine, trapped in between my Kevlar vest and polyester shirt. I was outside the car waiting on a wrecker to come to tow the vehicle. I was preoccupied with filling out a Recovered Stolen Vehicle Report. When I checked the car, believe it or not, the steering column was *not* damaged. Usually a good indicator of a stolen vehicle is a damaged steering column.

I concluded that whoever stole this car *had* to have the keys on him. Cases like these usually turn out to be a "breach of trust" where someone borrowed a car and didn't return it on time. More times than not, the frustrated owner will report it to the police as "stolen."

Well, about ten minutes went by before the wrecker service showed up. The tow truck driver got out and looked over the stolen car. He noticed that the brake was on and he wanted to pop the door lock open with a Slim Jim. My Field Training Officer (FTO) and I looked at each other and I said, "Do what you have to do."

An alarm went off as soon as the tow truck driver opened the locking mechanism. My FTO said, "Close the door and let's wait." I said to myself, *"What kind of an idiot steals a car and then sets the alarm on to 'arm' a stolen car?"* Sure enough, an apartment door opened up and I saw this disheveled guy rubbing the crud out of his eyes. You could tell that he had just woken up from a long night of partying.

"Hey! Why don't you get the keys to this car and turn off the alarm?" my FTO said to this fella. "People are trying to sleep around here!" he added.

The man said, "Okay, sir." Then he went back into the apartment for about 30 seconds looking for the keys. He returned to the door and walked outside wearing his shorts and house shoes. As soon as he put the key into the car door to open up the vehicle, I arrested him for "Possession of a Stolen Motor Vehicle."

I later learned that this thief saw the car at a gas station in Connecticut and he took off in the new car while the owner was inside shopping. He drove it all the way down to South Carolina and ended up at this rundown, old apartment complex. It was like a shiny penny lying in the dirt. This was a great day at work and we were off looking for more things to get into as soon as the car had been towed off of the lot.

Eggs Make a Dog's Coat Shiny

I was living in Florence, South Carolina and was just getting to know the area. I was with the South Carolina State Police. I had not lived there very long and I was meeting new people every day. Everyone knew that I was from Indiana and they made fun of me. They would call me a "Damn Yankee," "Yankee this" and "Yankee that." It was all that I heard for a while.

I was getting tired of the name calling. As cops, we often try to pass long periods of boredom by playing jokes on people. Most of the time, I was on the receiving end. Boy, did I ever get my share of pranks. I was trying to come up with some new things that I could do to my new friends. I didn't want to be mean, but I wanted to be heard.

So, one day I decided to get even with a deputy who worked on the drug unit. He was a K9 handler and a great guy. He was a hard worker and I used to make a lot of drug cases with him and his team. I was at home one night and I just went to the grocery store. I had bought a carton of eggs and when I got home I realized that I already had a couple dozen in the refrigerator. Then it hit me!

I hardboiled two dozen eggs and took them to work the next day. When we were all lined up I told the other guys what I was going to do. We were all in tears laughing. I told my buddies that as soon as our K9 officer stopped a car they should go "back" him up and I'd feed his dog the hardboiled eggs. Everything was all set to go…so we waited.

Sure enough, a little bit later, the K9 officer stopped a motorist for a traffic violation. A couple of us went down to back him up. As soon as we pulled over, I grabbed the twenty-four eggs and I was off to the K9 officer's car. I could see the K9 officer talking to the violator about the traffic infraction. He wasn't looking back at me.

"Here doggie, doggie." One egg down… two eggs down… and then before you'd know it, he had gulped twenty-four eggs down the hatch.

As soon as we all were cleared, we set back up in the middle of the interstate. We parked window to window…and it didn't take long!

The canine let a big one…and it was loud! "Damn!" The K9 handler yelled at the dog, "That smells like rotten eggs!"

I could barely hold it together and neither could the rest of the guys. Then again, again, and again. The dog was ripe with the odor of rotten eggs.

The K9 handler said to us, "Maybe I should give the dog a break and walk him." So the K9 handler got out of his car and walked his dog around in the wooded area of the median. I was laughing so hard. I could see the dog doing the duck crawl and laying down pile after pile and he had really bad gas.

All of the guys and I were crying from laughing so hard.

The K9 handler never found out what we did to his canine until two years later when I told him at a law enforcement function. The dog was retired a year after this event. He had cancer, but he sure did have a shiny coat! This was a great dog and he was outstanding at finding dope. May he rest in peace.

The Damn Yankee Strikes Again

After I was hired by the South Carolina Department of Public Safety I had to go back to the police academy to be certified to do commercial vehicle safety inspections. The state doubled us up in rooms at the academy. It was not a good place to go back to, especially after you've already graduated. Once you leave, you never really want to go back. Well, they roomed me up again with a guy from the Deep South. His family had been in South Carolina before the Civil War. Well, here we go again with calling me "Yankee." As if I hadn't heard it enough while living down there for nineteen years.

My roommate was named "Shawn" and he lived upstate near Greenville. He arrived at the academy with his nice, big suitcase. He introduced himself and bragged about how he was the "man of his house" and his wife did everything for him. She cooked, cleaned, washed, ironed and folded his clothes. She did just about everything that he demanded.

The evidence was clear that he was right. When he opened up his suitcase, I could see that everything inside it had been cleaned and pressed. His clothes were ironed and even had military creases.

Wow, he was the king of his castle for sure! No denying that. I was impressed that his wife had done everything for him.

All week long, the guys would hang out in the hallways and rooms, talking to each other and sharing stories. It just so happened that at the academy, we were not allowed visitors and we couldn't leave. We were away from home and our loved ones. One night I heard something slide under our door. I yelled at Shawn, "Hey! What's that?" He got up and turned the light on and it was a stack of girly magazines. This was a pretty good batch; Pam Anderson debuted in one of those magazines.

Well, what I didn't tell you was that Shawn was very religious… and his wife was even more pious. So, here was the reverent Shawn thumbing through these filthy magazines, flipping through cover to cover before ever putting them down. He looked at one after another for several hours straight. Eventually, I turned my light off to go to sleep and later that night when I woke up to turn over, Shawn was still looking at the magazines. He was now reading the articles…and it was past three in the morning.

Well, a few weeks had passed since that night and the stack of magazines were still in our room. I even think that a few more were slid to us under the door. Even after several weeks of rooming with Shawn, he still made fun of me for being a Yankee. Also, every chance that he got to poke fun at anyone, he did. He sure put it out there and he enjoyed spreading the "love" around to everyone.

On the morning that we were to get our certificates, I was about to leave for the classroom. Shawn asked me if I wanted the magazines and I told him, "No thanks." I said to him, "Why don't you keep them?" He laughed and said that his wife would kill him if she ever found them. So, he got into the shower and I told him that I'd throw them away. On the way out of the room I said, "See you in a little bit." He replied, "Okay, Yankee Boy."

I stopped in my tracks and looked over at his suitcase. His shirts were all folded up and lying there nice and neat. The clothes were stacked almost to the top and I guess that all that was missing was his shower bag. I took all of the dirty magazines and stuffed them under the bottom layer of his clothes. Then I walked out and said, "Yankee Boy is out of here."

After class, I drove back to Hilton Head Island where I lived. That night, about seven in the evening, I got a phone call. It was Shawn!

I could hear, in the background, something that sounded as if the devil was being cast out of someone with all of the biblical quotes being thrown around. I even heard something like, "You brought

this garbage into my house, you sick pervert, you!"
Then I heard the infamous accusation, "You'd rather
be with this than with me!"

Oh boy, it was ugly! Shawn said to me, "Man,
you've got to tell my wife the truth and let her know
that these are not mine!" I said, "Okay, put her on
the phone and I'll tell her the truth." She answered
the phone with a devilish hello.

"Hello, I was Shawn's roommate at the
academy and those magazines are *not* mine! They're
his!"

She hung up on me and that was it. About a
month later, we all had to go to the firing range to
shoot and look who pulled up with his tail between
his legs. It was Shawn!

I said, "Hey!" and he told me that he didn't
think that what I did was too funny. He went on to
tell me that he had to sleep on the couch for about
three weeks until she let him back into his own
bedroom. This story was told again that day to all of
my friends. Once again, we shared a laugh at his
expense. Those were the days!

Point Me in the Right Direction

One night I had the honor of having the
Director of the Department of Public Safety do a ride
along with me. I was so honored. I had just seen him
at an award ceremony where I won the State Police
Officer of the Year Award for the second time. He
knew me and he'd always said to me in passing, "I

want to come ride with you one day to see how you guys make drug cases." I'd always answer, "Anytime."

Well, one night the Director showed up at a law enforcement network meeting. The meeting lasted for about thirty minutes and afterwards we left the gathering to go out to work in a group task force. It didn't matter to us if we were city, county, or state officers. Together, we'd work certain areas of the county to hit the high crime problem areas that we learned about from our intelligence and service calls.

I lived in Hilton Head and I didn't really know the area that we were working all that well. The reason being was that I was the only officer who lived in Hilton Head and was only permitted to work that area. So, the night that the Director came to me and said, "I'm riding with you tonight, if that's okay?" What would you say to your boss?

"Absolutely," I said. I thought to myself, *"Maybe I can impress him and one day I might just go up the ladder in my career."* It never hurts to shine when the brass is around… right?

Well, my partner got a drug case and a gun. The people he stopped in the car tried to bail out and run so you can just imagine the radio blaring with excitement. My partner, "Sugar Shane" called it out as "Highway 17, just south of Walterboro." The Director said, "Let's go!"

So we're cruising along and I'm going 55 mph, like I should when the Director is onboard.

We're talking and talking and we're fifteen minutes into the drive and we're not there yet. Everyone is arriving at the scene but me and the Director! The Director said to me, "How much farther?" I answered, "We should've been there by now!"

I called my partner, "Sugar Shane," and he corrected me by saying, "No, Highway 17 Alternate." There are two highways coming out of the same town and someone named them both "Highway 17."

Who does this? Only in the South do they do this! So, I had to backtrack and we're now thirty minutes away from all of the excitement. The Director said to me, "I don't have too much time." He had to drive all the way back to Columbia that night. The drive to Columbia from Walterboro is about a ninety minute drive.

The director said to me as I'm going 55 mph again like I should, "It wouldn't hurt my feelings if you got us there a little quicker." By the time he said that, we were there in no time… and safely. We got there just in time to see what was going on. There were a lot of "atta-boys." Then he said to me, "Take me back to my car."

The Director had a wonderful time. We were able to catch up on life stories and he was able to see all of the guys working together. What a great night to have good company and excitement. However, I can't believe that my one shot to make a great appearance, I got lost. I never did get promoted, but I never really wanted to because I loved being a road officer. I have no regrets.

It's Not Delivery

My partner Shane and I used to eat out a lot. We enjoyed each other's company. We were like brothers. He was the first person that I met when I moved down to Hilton Head. He came out and met me and the moving truck and helped me get settled. I didn't know him from Adam.

Many years into my career, Shane and I had pretty much seen just about everything. We had experienced a lot. We both traveled around the world teaching criminal interdiction. One of my favorite memories of working with him was the night we were sitting at a local Italian establishment. He and I split a pizza and some appetizers. It was so delicious that we were fighting over the last piece. Naturally, he got the last slice and was gloating about it. "Oh, this is sooooo good," he said as he rubbed it in.

After dinner, we had about two hours left on our shift. We wanted to grab one more case and then work our way back home. We didn't want to work the interstate, so we went into the inner-city for a little change in pace. Boy, did we ever get a change of pace this night.

As we drove down a side road to turn around, we witnessed a carjacking in progress. The driver was pulled out, hit in the head, and thrown into the backseat. I pulled up and cut the three guys off and jumped out of my car and drew my weapon down on the three subjects. I pinned them down and within a few seconds "Sugar Shane" pulled up and was out with me. We arrested and handcuffed the three men for "carjacking." I walked back to my car and that's when everything changed.

One of the men that we'd arrested was a high school track star in North Charleston. He took off running in a full sprint while still wearing the handcuffs. I yelled at Shane to go get him. Shane turned around and slid face first on the pavement and then he got up and the chase was on. I stayed behind and secured the two other subjects. Sugar Shane ran three blocks and caught this kid in somebody's yard. People started coming out of their houses. Here was Shane, huffing and puffing, with a whole stomach full of pizza. Remember he got the last piece. I'm so glad that he did. He enjoyed it so much that he got to taste it twice.

Sugar Shane, I miss those days. Remember that this is my book and this is how I remember it.

Swedish Bikini Team

Well, Shane and I used to also tease each other a lot. He was so fun to get because he never thought that I'd play tricks on him. Well, I talked to my boss about going to a conference in Chicago, Illinois and I wanted Shane to go with me. I pled a good case for us to get more training, and we were approved. We were going to the Windy City.

Since we were so late getting approval for the conference the host hotel no longer had any available rooms. We were going, but we had to stay at another location. This is not good!

Come to find out, every room was booked downtown except for a five star hotel. It was $400 a night and we were going to be there for a week. However, we were approved to stay at this hotel.

The name of the hotel was the "Swissotell." I looked up the hotel online and I was excited. I called Shane and told him about how great this hotel was going to be and he was riding on cloud nine. I went on to tell him that I looked at the scheduled events for that week and the Swedish Bikini Team was going to do a photo shoot the week that we were there. He was crying with joy and said he was a big fan. He was like a little kid on Christmas morning and he couldn't wait. This was all that he talked about and the "what if's" for about three weeks.

We made the drive up from Charleston to Chicago in less than twelve hours (I wish that I was kidding). As soon as we arrived, I checked us into the hotel. Shane was walking around the lobby and checking the board for scheduled events. I remember that he walked over to me and said, "Hey! I don't see anything about the Swedish Bikini Team here." I said, "Do you really think that they'd put up a sign in the hotel announcing it?" He agreed with me and said, "Yeah, I guess you're right."

As soon as we checked in and put our bags away, Shane went cruising the hallways. He started on the top floor and went from floor to floor, checking each wing, hallway, workout area, and the pool. He came back to the room looking all sad. I told him, "Don't worry, you'll see them walking around, eating, or something.

Each day after the training classes we'd return to our hotel and Shane would throw on some cologne and hit the hallways again. He even went down to the front desk and asked the clerk if he knew where the Swedish Bikini Team was hiding. The guy gave Shane a look like, "What are you talking about?" The clerk said that he didn't know where they were. Poor Shane!

When he came back to the room he said that no one would tell him where the photo shoot was taking place. Finally, I had to come clean about my prank and tell him that I got him. It was like letting the air out of a balloon. He confessed to me that he really had his hopes up. He was mad at me for the rest of that day. Nonetheless, I did enjoy seeing my buddy walk around with a little pep in his step, a little swagger to his walk. This was priceless!

Happy Anniversary

I have to say that this is my best story yet. My friend "Sugar Shane" lived in Walterboro, South Carolina. He'd often drive to Charleston for lots of things. Groceries, dinners, movies and shopping were all within a thirty minute drive. They have stores in Walterboro, but Charleston has more shopping.

In the middle of these two cities the cell phone signal is not too good. So halfway between the two, you couldn't get any calls. There was a dead zone near Cottageville and this was the route that he'd normally take.

One day, he told me it was his anniversary and he had plans to go to a Japanese steak house with his wife. He told me that the two of them were going to dress up and enjoy the night together. The reservation he made was for 9:00 pm. This place booked up very fast and he took what they had. He was really excited because this restaurant had been on TV several times and is famous.

Well, that night I needed to ask him a question so I called him around 8:15ish. The phone went right to voice mail, so I left him a message that I'll never forget. I said in broken English, "Mr. Shane, this is the owner of the restaurant and I'm very sorry, but I had to cancel your reservation." I said this in my best Japanese voice. I made it sound perfect, just like I was the owner. I told Shane that they had a large group of people and could no longer honor their dinner plans. I also told him again, in my best voice, that he could come back in a few days and I'd give him a coupon for ten percent off of his dinner. I closed by saying, "Sorry for the inconvenience that this might have caused."

I actually thought when he got the message that he'd recognize that it was me and have a good laugh. I forgot about it afterwards. So, when Shane and his bride got out of the "dead zone," he saw that had one missed message. He quickly called his phone to check his message. Sadly, he discovered that his dinner plans were cancelled. He really believed that it was the business owner, so he pulled over to the side of the road to break the bad news to his spouse. He told her that their reservations had been canceled.

Let me paint the picture better for you. It's almost nine in the evening on a Friday night. The two of them are all decked out in their best evening clothes with no place to go on their anniversary.

That Monday morning he came into work and was dejected. He was upset about his terrible weekend. I asked him what was wrong (I didn't know what happened). I was sure that he knew it was me who had called him and played a prank. I began feeling guilty as he shared with me about how his anniversary was a bust. He confided that he had a bad weekend and it all started with the dinner plans! He said that they didn't get to go to the Japanese steak house and ended up eating at Captain D's.

He played the message in front of all the guys about his dinner plans being canceled. I have to admit that it didn't sound like me either. I was agreeing with him. Then he said that he and his wife got into a huge argument.

It took me two years before I told him that it was me. I also waited until he was divorced before telling him. He and I laughed until we cried. Now he thinks that I did him a big favor. I believe that he's right. At least I was his best man in his next wedding. He and his bride were married at exactly 4:20 in the afternoon. Happy Anniversary!

It Was a Truck I Was Hiding Behind

I was involved in a high speed pursuit when I worked in Hilton Head. I was patrolling Jasper County on Highway 17 when I saw this car coming towards me. It was traveling in the triple digits. I tried turning around on the car as soon as the driver passed by me. I tried to make up the distance and soon enough I was close.

This driver pulled down a dirt road and a big dust storm had spread all over the road. I still followed him, but the visibility was not the best. Then I noticed a flash. The driver was running and he went and hid behind a truck. It was like playing "hide-and-seek" with a three year old. His concealment wasn't the best but he thought that I couldn't see him. He might as well have been holding up a sign that said, "Right here, here I am!" I parked my car and ran over and arrested him.

He tried telling me that it wasn't him. Really! He wasn't the guy wearing the same red ball cap and the same blue hooded jacket? He wasn't the same guy who left the door open and ran in front of my car and hid behind a truck?

So, I charged the driver with "speeding" and "failure to stop for blue lights" and "no driver's license." I booked him in the county jail and the entire time he kept insisting that I had the wrong guy. I must have made a mistake and that he was just working on his truck at an address where he didn't live… but it gets better!

Well, the court day came and he was not represented by a lawyer. He pled "not guilty." So the judge swore me and the driver in. I started the trial off and went into detail about the whole event. I was very thorough about the case and even presented video of him running in front of my car. I went on to say that he ran off and hid behind a "car" from me. He quickly jumped up and said, "It's wasn't a 'car' that I was hiding behind. It was a truck!"

I looked at the judge and said, "Yes, he's correct. It was a truck and not a car. I rest my case."

He had a look on his face like *"Yeah! I just got off of these charges."* He had no idea that he had just told on himself.

Guilty!

You have to love when they do the stupid things that they do. We have the best job in the world!

About the Authors

James Eagleson

James Eagleson is a highly trained officer in the field of criminal interdiction. He is from Evansville, Indiana. After high school he enlisted in the U.S. Navy. James was assigned to the *USS John Rodgers* out of Charleston, South Carolina. His service to his country took him to many different countries as a member of the Combat Systems Division. James spent six months assigned to law enforcement operations in the Caribbean Sea. The primary mission was seizing contraband from go-fast boats. After serving his four years, he was given an honorable discharge.

James began his career in law enforcement when he was hired by the North Charleston, SC Police Department. After a little over a year he moved on to work for the South Carolina Department of Public Safety. He worked as an interdiction officer on the I-95 corridor. After several years on the State's Drug Unit, he was assigned a K9 Officer position. James's work as a proactive commercial vehicle enforcement officer resulted in numerous major seizures of contraband.

In 2001, James was named Police Officer of the Year by three different agencies (the South

Carolina Department of Public Safety, the South Carolina Department of Revenue, and the South Carolina Department of Transportation). In 2003, James was nominated as the South Carolina Department of Public Safety Commissioned Officer of the Year. In 2004, James was named the South Carolina State Police Officer of the Year.

For five years James was assigned part time to Project SeaHawk as a task force officer with the Department of Justice. His duties were border checks on commercial vehicles in the port of Charleston as well as boarding container ships that entered the harbor.

James was certified by the South Carolina Criminal Justice Academy as a police instructor. At the academy level he has taught criminal interdiction tactics. James has been an interdiction instructor at the national level teaching for prestigious entities such as the Drug Interdiction Assistance Program (DIAP). James has taught hundreds of classes for the Drug Enforcement Administration, Northeast Counterdrug Training Center, Regional Counterdrug Training Center, HIDTA, including instructing at Advanced Agent Training in Quantico, Virginia. He has also taught at the U.S. Border Patrol Academy in Artesia, New Mexico.

After he retired from the South Carolina State Police, James founded The 420 Group where he is the Director of Training. The 420 Group teaches classes on Criminal Interdiction throughout the country. This criminal interdiction training has benefited thousands of officers from the federal, state, county and local level. James continues to pursue his passion - instructing law enforcement officers on the topic of criminal interdiction- and has logged thousands of hours of instruction.

While teaching for The 420 Group, he has also produced five professional training DVDs on concealment methods. He has also designed the first ever training program on Recreational Vehicles.

In 2012, he took The 420 Group international when he taught interdiction in Europe and Asia. The countries they have taught in include: Serbia, Bosnia, Macedonia, Albania, Moldova, and Mongolia. He supervised a team to work the border in Bosnia and labored alongside and trained Customs Officers from three countries. James has now traveled to all 50 States in the U.S.A. and to over 48 countries in his travels both teaching and serving his country.

As the Director of Training, he has built the very first ever law enforcement resort for police officers in Western Montana. He is a networker and enjoys being around the people who make this the best profession in the world.

In February of 2014 James became an author with the publication of *It's 4:20 Somewhere*. This is a complete guide to working Commercial Vehicle Interdiction.

Sam Smith

Sergeant Sam Smith is a nineteen-year veteran of the Evansville (Indiana) Police Department (EPD). He worked in Motor Patrol for five years as a patrol officer and a Field Training Officer (FTO). He was assigned to Personnel and Training as the Fitness Coordinator for three years. He was later transferred to the Field Training Unit (FTU) and worked as the FTU Coordinator. He was EPD's FTO of the Year (2005)

He was the head defensive tactics instructor for the EPD for six years. He holds black belts in Judo, Japanese Jujitsu, and Russian Sambo. He's won six state championships in Judo and was Indiana's first Brazilian Jujitsu state champion (1997). Smith was also the first Hook-n-Shoot Grappling Champion (1998) and he won the Tristate Superheavyweight Submission Fighting Championship in 1999. He was voted by his peers as Indiana's Judo "Competitor of the Year" (2002). He stopped competing in 2005.

Sergeant Smith was one of the founders of the South Western Indiana Law Enforcement Academy (SWILEA) where he taught a variety of topics as well as being the academy's fitness officer and the lead defensive tactics instructor. He was promoted to sergeant in 2006 and has worked as a Motor Patrol Supervisor, Adult Investigations Sergeant, and Financial Crimes Sergeant. He's currently the FTU Sergeant. Presently, he's the Less Lethal Force Supervisor and oversees the Firearms Unit.

Sergeant Smith is an avid writer. This is his third book in five years. He has a forthcoming book that's scheduled to be published in the Philippines about international terrorism and the history of Christian Muslim relationships in Southeast Asia. He wrote a defensive tactics manual for SWILEA and he has approximately 30 articles about radical Islam, the Nation of Islam, and police subculture that have been published online. He has recently had several articles published in *Tactical Response* and *Law and Order Magazine.*

He holds two degrees, a Bachelor's and a Master's, from Indiana University, Bloomington Indiana. Sergeant Smith is a former adjunct professor with the University of Southern Indiana. For fifteen years, he taught a variety of subjects for the Department of Sociology until he was promoted to Sergeant and was assigned to second shift. He's been married for over twenty-two years. He's the father of a teenage son (Nate) and a teenage daughter (Annie) and he has a feisty, little Jack Russell Terrier named "Hercules."

Made in the USA
Columbia, SC
23 May 2019